101 Nutrition Tips for People with Diabetes

Patti B. Geil, MS, RD, FADA, CD
Lea Ann Holzmeister, RD, CDE

Viva Books

New Delhi | Mumbai | Chennai | Kolkata | Bangalore | Hyderabad | Kochi | Guwahati

First Indian Edition 2004
Reprinted 2005, 2007, 2008

VIVA BOOKS PRIVATE LIMITED

- 4737/23 Ansari Road, Daryaganj, New Delhi 110 002
  E-mail: vivadelhi@vivagroupindia.net, Tel. 42242200
- 76, Service Industries, Shirvane, Sector 1, Nerul, Navi Mumbai 400 706
  E-mail: vivamumbai@vivagroupindia.net, Tel. 27721273, 27721274
- Jamals Fazal Chambers, 26 Greams Road, Chennai 600 006
  E-mail: vivachennai@vivagroupindia.net, Tel. 28290304, 28294241
- B-103, Jindal Towers, 21/1A/3 Darga Road, Kolkata 700 017
  E-mail: vivakolkata@vivagroupindia.net, Tel. 22836381, 22816713
- 7, Sovereign Park Apartments, 56-58, K. R. Road, Basavanagudi, Bangalore 560 004
  E-mail: vivabangalore@vivagroupindia.net, Tel. 26607409, 26607410
- 101-102 Mughal Marc Apartments, 3-4-637 to 641, Narayanguda, Hyderabad 500 029
  E-mail: vivahyderabad@vivagroupindia.net, Tel. 27564481, 27564482
- First Floor, Beevi Towers, SRM Road, Kaloor, Kochi 682 018, Kerala
  E-mail: vivakochi@vivagroupindia.net, Tel: 0484-2403055, 2403056
- H. No. 12, P. B. Road, Rehabari, Near Arya Hospital, Guwahati 781 008
  E-mail: vivaguwahati@vivagroupindia.net, Tel: 0361-2735624

www.vivagroupindia.com

Published by arrangement with

American Diabetes Association
1701 North Beauregard Street
Alexandria, Virginia 22311

The suggestion and information contained in this publication are generally consistent with the *Clinical Practice Recommendations* and other policies of the American Diabetes Association, but they do not represent the policy or position of the Association or any of its boards or committees. Reasonable steps have been taken to ensure the accuracy of the information presented. However, the American Diabetes Association cannot ensure the safety or efficacy of any product or service described in this publication. Individuals are advised to consult a physician or other appropriate health care professional before undertaking any diet or exercise program or taking any medication referred to in this publication. Professionals must use and apply their own professional judgement, experience, and training and should not rely solely on the information contained in this publication before prescribing any diet, exercise, or medication. The American Diabetes Association —its officers, directors, employees, volunteers, and members—assumes no responsibility or liability for personal or other injury, loss or damage that may result from the suggestions or information in this publication.

ISBN-10: 81-309-1189-2
ISBN-13: 978-81-309-1189-2

Published by Vinod Vasishtha for Viva Books Private Limited, 4737/23, Ansari Road, Daryaganj, New Delhi - 110 002. Printed and bound by Anand Sons, Delhi - 110 092.

Dedication

To our families

Jeff, Erin, Adam, and Emily Holzmeister
Jack, Kristen, and Rachel Geil
101 thank-yous for your love and support!

–Lea Ann and Patti

TABLE OF CONTENTS

Chapter 1
NUTRITION: THE BIG PICTURE

How do I know when I should see a registered dietitian?

▼
TIP:

See a registered dietitian (RD) when your diabetes is first diagnosed, when a new doctor changes your treatment plan, or twice a year for a routine review of your meal plan and goals. See the RD more often if

- You want to improve diabetes control
- Your lifestyle or schedule changes, such as a new job, marriage, or pregnancy
- Your nutritional needs keep changing (children)
- You've begun an exercise program or had a change in diabetes medication
- You feel bored, frustrated, or unmotivated to use your meal plan
- You have unexplained high and low blood glucose levels
- You're concerned about weight or blood fat levels
- You develop nutrition-related complications, such as high blood pressure or kidney disease

You may have an RD on your diabetes team. Ask your doctor or hospital for a referral. You can call the American Diabetes Association (800/342-2383), The American Dietetic Association (800/366-1655), or the American Association of Diabetes Educators (800/832-6874) for referrals. Many RDs are certified diabetes educators (CDE) and have additional training in diabetes care.

What should I eat until I can meet with the registered dietitian?

▼
TIP:

Eat the foods that are healthy for everyone—grains, beans, vegetables, fruits, low-fat milk, and meat. Cut down on foods and drinks with a lot of added sugar (soda, desserts, candy) and fat (fried foods, lunch meats, gravy, salad dressings). You do not need special or diet foods.

It is important to eat about the same amount of food at the same time each day. Don't eat one or two large meals. Try to eat at least three small meals each day, especially if you are taking diabetes medication. You may need a snack between meals and before you go to bed. Avoid drinking alcohol until you learn how it fits into your diabetes treatment plan. Remember, you can make a big difference in your diabetes control through what you choose to eat. Before you see the RD, keep a record of everything you eat and drink for 3–5 days and bring this record to your appointment. This will help the RD personalize the meal plan to you.

How often do I need to eat for good diabetes control?

▼
TIP:

This depends on the type of diabetes you have, your medications, physical activity, and where your blood glucose level is at the moment. An RD can help you decide.

For type 1 or type 2 using insulin: Have food in your system when your insulin is peaking. You may need three meals and an evening snack. If you take two injections of short- and intermediate-acting insulin, you may need three meals and three snacks. If you use Humalog, eat within 15 minutes of taking your insulin. You may need a snack for physical activity (see p. 61). A common mistake is not waiting 1/2 hour after taking regular insulin to eat. If you start eating before insulin activity is peaking, you have higher blood glucose levels after meals.

For type 2: Eat a small meal every 2–3 hours. When you eat smaller amounts of food, your blood glucose levels are lower after eating. Mini-meals spread over the day may help control your hunger and calorie intake, leading to better blood glucose control and weight loss. Your blood cholesterol levels will also be lower.

What can I eat for snacks?

▼
TIP:

Choose from the same healthy foods that you eat at meals. Often, snacks are based on foods with 15 grams of carbohydrate per serving. Good snack choices begin at the bottom of the food pyramid. Choose foods from the grain group, such as air-popped popcorn, baked tortilla chips and salsa, graham crackers, pretzels, bagels, or cereal. Fresh fruits and vegetables make excellent snacks, and they're also portable! To make a snack more substantial, add a source of low-fat protein, such as low-fat milk, reduced-fat peanut butter on a slice of bread or a bagel, low-fat cheese on crackers, or a slice of turkey breast on whole wheat bread.

Be prepared! Always carry a snack with you in case of a delayed meal or unexpected change in your schedule. Snacks can be stashed in your desk, briefcase, backpack, or glove compartment. Having good food on hand will save you from hypoglycemia and from having to settle for less nutritious fast foods.

How can keeping a food diary help my diabetes?

▼
TIP:

The food you eat raises your blood glucose. Until you write it down, you probably are not aware of how much or what you are eating. A food diary helps you make important decisions about your medication, meal plan, and exercise plan.

- Record information you need. If you want to lose weight, measure your serving sizes, and write down how many calories or fat grams you're getting for several days. Looking up the nutrient values of foods helps you learn what nutrients each food gives you.
- Keep records that are easy to use—a notebook, calendar, or form created on your computer. Write it down when you eat it; don't wait until later.
- Use the information. Bring your record to the next appointment with your RD. Look for patterns in your eating behaviors and blood glucose levels. For example, your records may show that high-fat snacks in late afternoon result in high blood glucose at dinner. You also notice that your lunch is much smaller than other meals and causes you to be too hungry before dinner. You may want to adjust the size of lunch and decrease your afternoon eating.

Why are serving sizes important? Is there an easy way to remember them?

▼
TIP:

No matter what meal plan you follow—carbohydrate counting, exchanges, or the food guide pyramid—serving size is the key. An extra ounce of meat or tablespoon of margarine doesn't sound like much, but it can quickly add up to higher blood glucose levels and weight gain.

Begin by using standard kitchen measuring cups, spoons, and food scales until you train your eyes to see correct serving sizes. Once you've weighed, measured, and looked at 1/2 cup of green beans or 5 oz of chicken, you'll have a mental picture no matter where you dine. Every few months, measure some servings again to keep your eyes sharp and your servings the right size.

Mental pictures can help you eat correct serving sizes.

Food	Looks like
1 cup pasta or rice	a clenched fist
1/2 cup vegetables	half a tennis ball
1 cup broccoli	a light bulb
3 oz meat, chicken, or fish	a deck of cards or palm of a woman's hand
1 oz cheese	two saltine crackers or a 1-inch square cube

What should I be looking for on food labels—carbohydrate or fat?

Nutrition Facts
Serving Size 1 cup (228g)
Servings Per Container 2

Amount Per Serving	
Calories 260 Calories from Fat 120	
	% Daily Value*
Total Fat 13g	20%
Saturated Fat 5g	25%
Cholesterol 30mg	10%
Sodium 660mg	28%
Total Carbohydrate 31g	10%
Dietary Fiber 0g	0%
Sugars 5g	
Protein 5g	
Vitamin A 4% • Vitamin C 2%	
Calcium 15% • Iron 4%	

* Percent Daily Values are based on a 2,000 calorie diet. Your daily values may be higher or lower depending on your calorie needs:

	Calories:	2,000	2,500
Total Fat	Less than	65g	80g
Sat Fat	Less than	20g	25g
Cholesterol	Less than	300mg	300mg
Sodium	Less than	2,400mg	2,400mg
Total Carbohydrate		300g	375g
Dietary Fiber		25g	30g

Calories per gram:
Fat 9 • Carbohydrate 4 • Protein 4

▼
TIP:

Most people with diabetes should be looking at both carbohydrate and fat on the Nutrition Facts panel on food labels. Carbohydrate is what raises your blood glucose the most, so it's important to you. Fat carries the most calories per gram, so it affects your weight. Also, diabetes puts you more at risk for developing heart disease. Eating foods lower in fat (especially saturated fat) may help you lose weight and lower your risk for heart disease.

The total amount of carbohydrate you eat affects your blood glucose. The carbohydrate listed in the Nutrition Facts can be from beans, vegetables, pasta, grains, and sugars (added or naturally present in foods such as milk and fruit). Keeping track of the total grams of carbohydrate you eat and drink is more important than where it came from. The food label will tell you exactly how many grams of carbohydrate and fat are in a serving of food.

How do I deal with comments such as "Are you allowed to eat that?"

▼

TIP:

Your family and friends mean well. When this happens,

- **Recognize your own feelings.** Part of adjusting to diabetes is recognizing the difficult emotions that come with it. How do you feel about the lifestyle changes and pressures of self-care?
- **Recognize the feelings of family and friends.** Your family and friends are also adjusting to your diabetes and the ways it affects them. They may feel anxious, intimidated, guilty, or overwhelmed.
- **Use positive reframing.** Change the way you see the situation. If you feel angry at someone's comment, take a moment to acknowledge your own feeling and then the other person's feeling. Then look at the situation in a positive way. For example, you may say, "Thanks for reminding me. I know you want to help. I've already planned to adjust my insulin (or exercise) to handle the additional calories and carbohydrate in this food."
- **Develop an interaction plan.** Changing years of old thinking and communication patterns takes time. In a calm moment, discuss a new way to talk about food and diabetes issues.

Now that sugar is no longer forbidden for people with diabetes, can I eat all the sweets I want?

▼
TIP:

It's true that the carbohydrate in table sugar has the same effect on your blood glucose as any other carbohydrate, such as that in bread, potatoes, or fruit. All carbohydrates, in equal amounts, will raise your blood glucose level the same way no matter what type of diabetes you have. For blood glucose control, focus on the total amount of carbohydrate you eat, rather than where it comes from. You substitute sweets into your meal plan for other carbohydrates—don't add them on top.

No, don't have sweets at every meal. Sugary foods don't have the nutrients, vitamins, and minerals that your body needs to be healthy. That's why we call these calories "empty" and list these foods in the top of the food pyramid. If you include sweets in a meal, eat a small serving, and check your blood glucose before and 1–2 hours after you eat to see how it affects you. Keep an eye on your weight and blood glucose levels over time. Hold back on the sweets if you see your numbers creeping up.

I went to lunch with three friends who also have diabetes. We all follow different types of meal plans. What happened to the "diabetic" diet?

▼
TIP:

Just as there is no one medication that works for all people with diabetes, there is no single meal-planning approach. The standard 1800-calorie preprinted diet sheet is gone. Individualization is the key to good diabetes control.

The best meal plans are designed by you and an RD and are based on your health, other medications, activity level, and treatment goals. Your friend with type 1 diabetes may be taking multiple insulin injections and using the carbohydrate counting approach with frequent blood glucose monitoring. Her food choices would be quite different from your friend with type 2 diabetes and high blood fat levels who needs to lose weight. She may be trying to lower her carbohydrate intake and increase the monounsaturated fats in her diet by eating more nuts, olives, or canola oil. And the friend who works swing shift is probably using an entirely different approach to the timing and food choices in her meals and snacks. The important thing is to use a meal plan that works for you.

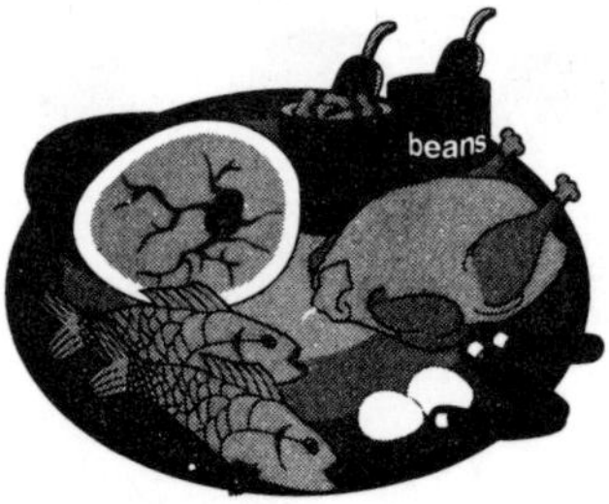

I've heard that a low-carbohydrate, high-protein, high-fat diet will help me lose weight without cutting calories. Should I change from the high-carbohydrate, low-fat diet I've always followed?

▼

TIP:

Probably not. A low-carbohydrate diet is very difficult to follow for a long period of time. On this diet, you eat meat, eggs, and cheese but very few carbohydrate foods, such as pasta, breads, fruits, and vegetables. You eat too few fruits and vegetables to get all the vitamins and minerals you need.

The rapid weight loss on a low-carbohydrate diet comes from an unhealthy loss of water and muscle tissue. Side effects include dehydration, low blood pressure, and increased work for the kidneys. The high fat certainly isn't good for heart health. Other side effects include constipation, fatigue, and nausea. And as with all very restricted diets, once you go back to a normal way of eating, your weight is going to come back.

Until there's more evidence, it's probably best to continue with a balanced carbohydrate meal plan. If you have insulin resistance, you may do better substituting some monounsaturated fats for carbohydrates (see p. 46). Get your health care team's help to decide on a nutrition approach for you.

Will fiber help my diabetes control?

▼
TIP:

Fiber can keep your blood glucose from going high after a meal because it slows down the speed at which the food is digested. A high-fiber, low-fat way of eating can also reduce your risk for cancer, cardiovascular disease, high blood pressure, and obesity. Fiber has a favorable effect on cholesterol, too.

Fiber in a food is made up of two types: insoluble fiber, such as that in vegetables and whole-grain products, and soluble fiber, found in fruits, oats, barley, and beans. Insoluble fiber improves gastrointestinal function, while soluble fiber can affect blood glucose and cholesterol. Unfortunately, most Americans eat only 8–10 grams of fiber daily, not the recommended 20–35 grams a day from a variety of foods. You can increase fiber by eating foods such as the ones in this chart.

Food	Serving Size	Total Fiber (g)	Soluble Fiber (g)
Beans	1/2 cup cooked	6.9	2.8
Oat bran	1/3 cup dry	4.0	2.0
Barley	1/4 cup dry	3.0	0.9
Orange, fresh	1 small	2.9	1.8
Oatmeal	1/3 cup dry	2.7	1.4

Is it true that beans can improve diabetes control?

▼
TIP:

Yes. Beans digest slowly, resulting in only a small rise in blood glucose and insulin levels. Several research studies have shown that eating 1 1/2–2 1/2 cups of cooked beans daily leads to beneficial effects on the control of diabetes. Beans also reduce the risk of cardiovascular disease, a common complication for people with diabetes. Eating 1–3 cups of cooked beans a day will lower total cholesterol in the range of 5–19%. Beans are also an excellent source of folate, which may reduce the risk of cardiovascular disease.

Packed with protein, fiber, vitamins, and minerals, beans are also low in fat, cholesterol, and sodium. They can be included in all types of diabetes meal plans. Beans can be used in salads, soups, or entrees. Canned beans require less preparation time and have the same beneficial effects as dried beans.

Soak dried beans overnight and rinse well before cooking. Introduce beans gradually into your diet, chew thoroughly, and drink plenty of liquids to aid digestion. Enzyme products such as "Beano" can also help you avoid gastrointestinal distress.

What is the difference between the Diabetes Food Pyramid and the USDA Food Pyramid?

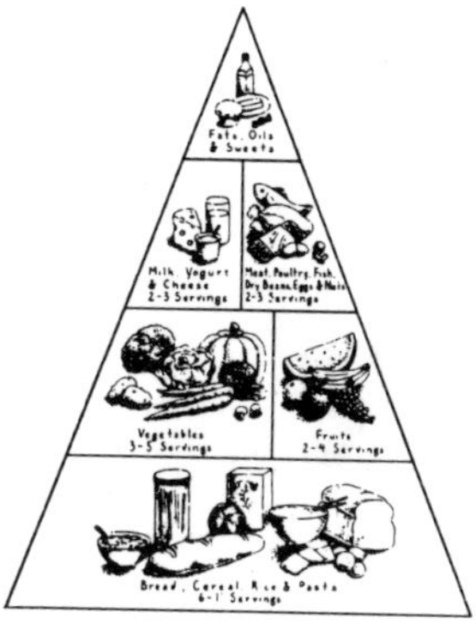

USDA Pyramid

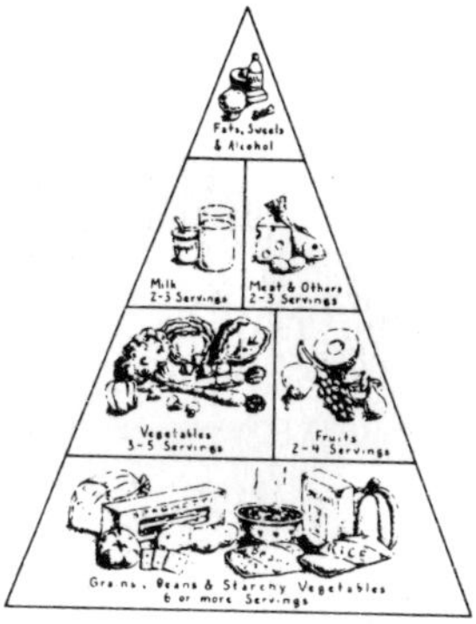

Diabetes Food Pyramid

▼

TIP:

The Diabetes Food Pyramid in *The First Step in Diabetes Meal Planning* is based on the USDA Food Guide Pyramid. There are only a few differences between the two pyramids. Each has six food groups, but the names are a little different. In the USDA Food Pyramid, cheese is in the Milk, Yogurt, and Cheese group, but in the Diabetes Food Pyramid, cheese is in the Meat and Others group. Cheese is mostly protein and fat, like foods found in the meat group. In the USDA Pyramid, beans are in the Meat group, but in the Diabetes Pyramid, beans are in Grains, Beans, and Starchy Vegetables because beans are a good source of carbohydrate and fiber. The food group at the tip of the Diabetes Pyramid includes alcohol with fats and sweets. This suggests limiting all three.

Both pyramids were designed to encourage you to include more foods in your diet from the largest groups—grains, beans and starchy vegetables, vegetables, and fruits—and fewer foods from the small groups at the top.

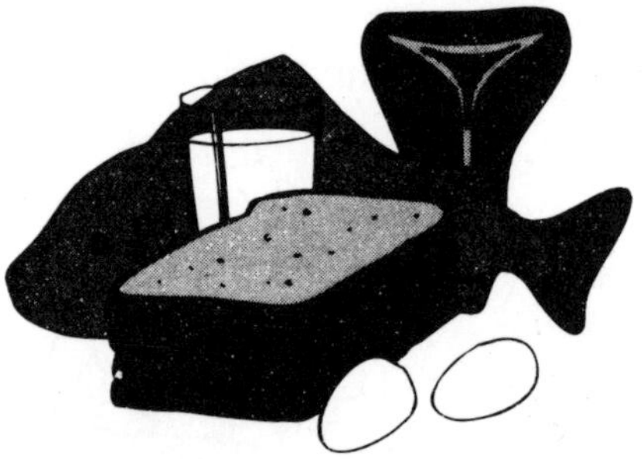

I keep hearing about carbohydrate counting. Is it still okay to use exchanges?

▼
TIP:

Yes. The exchange system is a valuable way for people with diabetes to plan meals. It can also help if you want to count carbohydrates. The *Exchange Lists for Meal Planning* group foods with similar carbohydrate content, so the "carb" counting is already done for you. For example, all the foods on the starch list (1 slice of bread, 3/4 cup cold cereal, etc.) contain 15 grams of carbohydrate.

To use exchanges, you need an individualized meal plan that tells you how many exchanges from each list to eat daily for meals and snacks. You can choose a variety of foods from the exchange lists to fit into your meal plan. An RD can help you design a meal plan and teach you how to use this system. In 1995 the *Exchange Lists* were updated. The food groupings were changed and more foods were included. A pocket-sized guide is now available.

Many people prefer to use exchanges because it helps keep their food choices balanced and healthy. If this system works for you, there is no reason to switch to another.

What is carbohydrate counting?

▼
TIP:

It is a precise method of meal planning for people with diabetes. Foods containing carbohydrate (grains, vegetables, fruit, milk, and sugar) have the largest effect on blood glucose level. A small amount of carbohydrate (1 apple) raises blood glucose some; a larger amount of carbohydrate (3 apples) raises blood glucose more. You track how the carbohydrate affects you by monitoring your blood glucose.

You have to invest some time in monitoring blood glucose, record keeping, measuring food servings, and learning about nutrients in foods. People with type 1 diabetes can determine the exact amount of insulin to take based on the amount of carbohydrate they eat. People with type 2 diabetes can benefit from eating consistent amounts of carbohydrate each day.

Carbohydrate counting has 3 levels: 1) eating consistent amounts of carbohydrate; 2) recognizing and managing patterns in blood glucose, food, medication, and exercise; and 3) intensive management of blood glucose. You may only need to learn about level 1. The amount of work may seem overwhelming at first, but most people find the improvements in blood glucose control are worth it! An RD can help you learn carbohydrate counting.

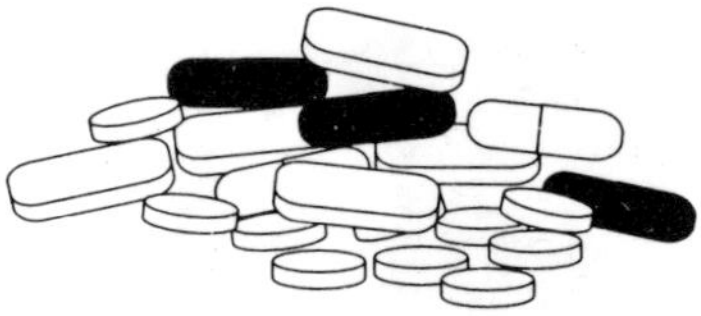

Do I need special vitamins and minerals because I have diabetes?

▼
TIP:

You don't need special vitamins because of diabetes. You do need vitamins and minerals for a well-functioning body, whether you have diabetes or not. If you are eating a variety of foods, you don't need a special vitamin or mineral supplement. There is currently no scientific evidence to show that certain vitamins or minerals can improve your blood glucose control, except in rare cases of deficiencies of the minerals chromium, copper, magnesium, manganese, selenium, or zinc. (See pp. 79–81.)

Discuss your diet with your physician or RD. You may need a vitamin and mineral supplement if you are

- On a diet of fewer than 1,200 calories a day
- Following a strict vegetarian diet
- At risk for bone disease
- Over age 65
- Pregnant or breastfeeding
- Taking diuretics

I really don't feel like eating in the morning. Do I have to eat breakfast?

▼

TIP:

Yes. Breakfast is crucial for people with diabetes. Your body has been without food for 8–12 hours. If you have type 1 diabetes, you need food to balance your injected insulin. If you have type 2 diabetes, you may skip breakfast to cut calories and lose weight, but it can lead to overeating later. In fact, research shows that breakfast skippers have higher blood cholesterol levels and extra pounds!

The best breakfast has carbohydrate, protein, and fiber. Save high-fat foods like bacon, sausage, and eggs for special occasions. You can choose cereal or an English muffin, low-fat milk or yogurt, and fruit, but there's no rule that says breakfast can't be pasta tossed with low-fat ricotta cheese or a leftover chicken breast with a piece of fruit.

Once you experience the dividends that breakfast pays in mood, performance, and diabetes control, you'll never skip your morning meal again!

Hint: People who eat a smaller evening meal (spread the calories out over the day) are more likely to wake up hungry for breakfast.

5

I've heard I'm supposed to eat five fruits and vegetables a day. Why?

▼
TIP:

Increasing the fruit and vegetables in your diet gives you better health, particularly in the prevention of cancer and heart disease. Fruits and vegetables are low in fat and are rich sources of vitamin A, vitamin C, and fiber. The average American eats only one serving of fruit and two servings of vegetables a day. You can find ways to put five or more servings in your salads, soups, sandwiches, main dishes, and snacks.

Fruits and vegetables affect diabetes in different ways. Fruit has 15 grams of carbohydrate per serving and affects your blood glucose within 2 hours. The amount blood glucose rises depends on whether you eat the fruit on an empty stomach, the form of the fruit (cooked or raw, whole or juice), and your blood glucose level when you eat. Check your blood glucose level after eating fruit to see what it does to you. Vegetables contain only 5 grams of carbohydrate per serving, few calories, and lots of vitamins and minerals. Moderate portions of vegetables have little effect on blood glucose but major effects on your health. Eat up!

Why does it seem that I need less food—and enjoy it less—now that I'm older?

▼
TIP:

If you are not as active as you were when you were younger, you probably don't need to eat as many calories. However, it may be that your appetite and enjoyment are being affected by one of the following changes in:

- Taste buds—affecting taste and interest in food
- Smell—affecting interest in food and the amount you eat
- Vision—making it difficult to read labels or recipes
- Hearing—affecting your ability to enjoy the social events around eating
- Touch—making it difficult to prepare food
- Teeth or poorly fitting dentures—making it painful to eat anything but soft, easy-to-chew foods

For reasons such as these, you may skip meals or eat fewer calories than you need, which affects your diabetes control. Limitations on movement can keep you from exercising, leading to loss of energy and appetite. Poor nutrition itself can bring on fatigue and a general sense of not feeling well. Work with your RD to overcome any challenges to following your meal plan.

Are plant sources of protein better for me than animal protein?

TIP:

Maybe. Plant proteins have benefits for people with diabetes. Plant foods are low in fat, especially saturated fat, and high in fiber. Animal protein adds cholesterol and saturated fat to our diets. People with diabetes have a greater risk of heart disease earlier in life. It is important to decrease saturated fat and cholesterol. For people with diabetic kidney disease, changing the source of protein in the diet as a treatment is being studied. Whether plant protein (beans, nuts, vegetables, tofu) is preferred over animal protein (meat, poultry, fish, milk, eggs) has not been decided. Discuss the latest research with your diabetes professionals. We do know that people in other countries who eat less meat and more soy protein and rice have fewer cancers and heart disease than Americans who eat lots of animal protein.

Animal protein contains all eight essential amino acids that you need to build cells in the body. Because your body can't make them, your food choices must supply them. However, eating a variety of plant proteins each day can also provide all the amino acids that you need (see p. 24).

Is there a benefit to including more soyfoods in my diet?

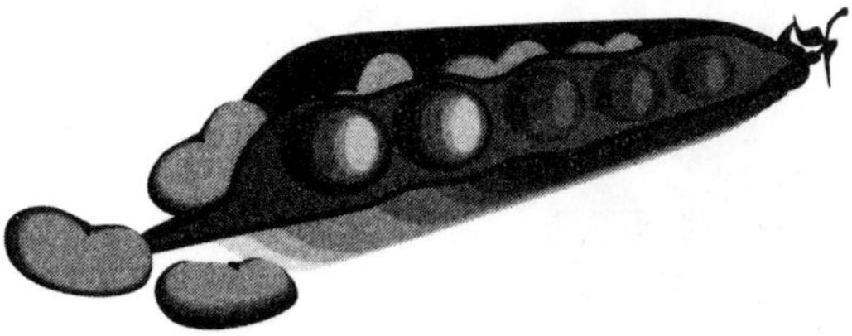

▼
TIP:

Yes. Soyfoods are low in saturated fat, have no cholesterol, and contain high quality protein. Scientists are learning about compounds in soybeans that may reduce your risk of certain chronic diseases like heart disease, osteoporosis, and cancer. Eating soyfoods may reduce blood cholesterol levels and decrease your risk for heart disease. In soy protein is a group of phytochemicals called isoflavones that may directly lower blood cholesterol levels. In certain stages of kidney disease, vegetable protein may be easier on the kidneys than animal protein.

Soybeans are made into a variety of foods, from ice cream to burgers, and they can be eaten whole or used in your recipes.

Soyfood (serving size)	Calories	Carbo-hydrate (g)	Protein (g)	Isoflavones (mg)
Soybeans (1/2 cup, cooked)	149	9	14	35
Tempeh (1/2 cup)	165	14	16	40
Tofu (1/2 cup)	94	2	10	40
Soynuts (1 oz)	128	9	11	40
Soy milk (1/2 cup)	40	2	3	40
Miso (2 Tbsp)	72	10	4	10

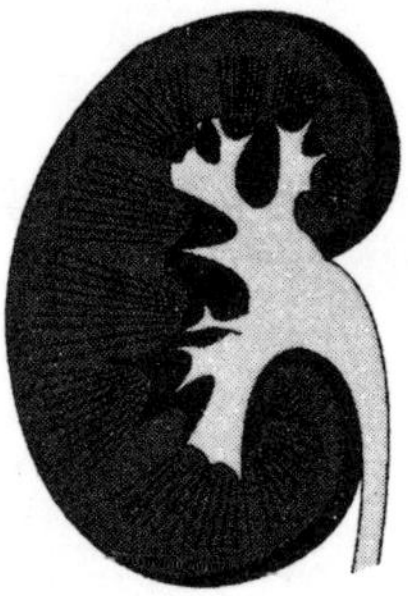

Should I eat less protein to keep my kidneys healthy?

▼
TIP:

Not necessarily. The American Diabetes Association (ADA) recommends that you eat the same amount of protein as the general public. The guidelines suggest eating 10–20% of calories as protein or 0.8 grams per kilogram for healthy adults. For a 60-kilogram (132-pound) person, this would be about 50 grams of protein per day. Some plant and animal protein choices are listed below. Most Americans eat more protein than they need. Eating extra protein makes kidneys work harder to get rid of protein waste products. If you already have kidney disease, you may want to eat less protein. Your doctor will consider the stage of kidney disease and your overall nutrition before prescribing a low-protein diet. Contact an RD for help.

Animal Proteins	Protein (g)
1 oz lean meat, poultry, or fish	7
1 cup milk or yogurt	8
1 egg	7

Plant Proteins	Protein (g)
1/2 cup cooked lentils, peas, or beans	7
2 Tbsp peanut butter	8
1/3 cup nuts	7
4 oz tofu	7
1 slice bread, 1/2 cup rice	2–3

Chapter 2
MANAGING MEDICATION

Do I need to eat snacks now that I'm taking diabetes pills?

TIP:

The way your pills work tells you whether you need snacks. Diabetes pills called sulfonylureas help the pancreas secrete insulin and can cause low blood glucose. If you take chlorpropamide (Diabinese), tolazamide (Tolinase), tolbutamide (Orinase), glipizide (Glucotrol or Glucotrol XL), glyburide (Glynase), or glimepiride (Amaryl), you probably need snacks, especially in the afternoon and evening.

Metformin (Glucophage) helps your body use insulin and decreases how much glucose your body makes and absorbs, so you don't need snacks.

Acarbose (Precose) delays absorption of glucose and does not cause hypoglycemia, so you don't need a snack. However, if you take acarbose with another diabetes medication and have low blood glucose, treat it with glucose tablets or milk instead of fruit (or sugar-sweetened) drinks. Acarbose slows the breakdown of sugar and may prevent your blood glucose from rising.

With troglitazone (Rezulin), snacks are not necessary. Rapaglinide (Prandin) helps the pancreas release insulin and is taken with meals or large (more than 250-calorie) snacks. Other snacks are not necessary.

If you take insulin injections and pills, you will probably need to eat healthy snacks.

Can I adjust my diet to avoid the side effects of acarbose (Precose)?

▼
TIP:

Acarbose is a pill for type 2 diabetes that slows down the digestion of carbohydrates. This helps lower your blood glucose level after a meal. It is often used along with another kind of diabetes pill and is taken three times a day with meals.

Acarbose may cause gas, diarrhea, and abdominal pain. This is because the carbohydrate you eat is not completely digested. It may help to increase the amount of medication slowly over a period of months. Eating a low-fiber diet may help. Avoid seeds, nuts, or beans. Select low-fiber cereals, breads, pasta, and rice. Peel and seed fruits and vegetables. It may also help to avoid gas-forming foods, such as beans and vegetables in the cabbage family. Other foods that may cause gas are milk, wheat germ, onions, carrots, celery, bananas, raisins, dried apricots, prune juice, and sorbitol. Sorbitol is a sugar alcohol used in dietetic or diabetic foods, such as sugar-free chewing gum, ice cream, candy, or cookies.

When you add fiber back to your diet, do it slowly and be sure to drink plenty of water.

My doctor wants me to start insulin, but I'm afraid I'll gain weight. How can I prevent weight gain while I'm taking insulin?

▼
TIP:

When your blood glucose is high, you lose calories as sugar in your urine. Taking insulin will give you better blood glucose control, which makes you feel better every day and lowers your chances of developing complications. This is important! However, when you stop losing calories in your urine, you can gain weight.

Review your eating habits, total calories, types of food, and how much fat and carbohydrate you eat with your RD. You may not need to eat as many calories, or you may need more exercise. This will help you take advantage of the more efficient job your body is doing at capturing and storing glucose.

There is another way that insulin can cause weight gain. If you take more insulin than you need, then you have to eat to "feed" the insulin and avoid low blood glucose. If you find yourself eating more than you want just to avoid hypoglycemia, your insulin dose may need adjusting. Discuss your medications, weight goal, and meal plan with your health care providers if you are concerned about gaining weight.

My doctor just switched my insulin to Humalog. How will this affect my blood glucose and meal plan?

▼
TIP:

You may have better blood glucose control and more flexible meal times. Humalog is a rapid-acting insulin that starts working within 10 minutes and peaks in 30–90 minutes, the way a normal pancreas responds to food. You may not need snacks between meals as you did with regular insulin, because Humalog does not stay in your body as long. You may need less Humalog than your regular insulin dose but more intermediate or long-acting insulin.

When you take Humalog and your blood glucose is in target range, you must eat within 15 minutes. This is quite different from waiting 30–45 minutes with regular insulin. If your blood glucose level is low before your meal, you might take Humalog after your meal.

It is easier to fine-tune your insulin dose to a meal with Humalog because it works only on the food eaten right then. Monitor your blood glucose levels when you begin using Humalog to learn how the medication works for you.

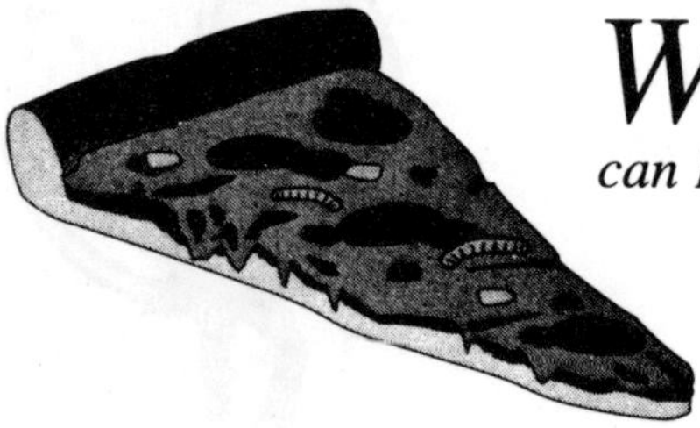

Whenever I eat pizza, my blood glucose level goes high. What can I do about that?

▼

TIP:

You might try eating a smaller serving. The type of crust, sauce, toppings, and size of slice varies a lot, so it is easy to overeat pizza. When you order pizza, ask for nutrition information. If you purchase it in the grocery store, check the Nutrition Facts panel. Exercising after you eat pizza can help bring down your blood glucose level.

For some people, high blood glucose occurs several hours after eating, perhaps because pizza is digested at different rates. Each person has a unique response to each food. Monitor your blood glucose up to 9 hours after eating pizza to find your response. If you take insulin, increasing premeal rapid-acting insulin may not be enough. Your intermediate or long-acting insulin may need an adjustment, also. Talk with your health care providers.

If you take diabetes pills, count the carbohydrates in your pizza serving. Is this more than you usually eat? Monitor blood glucose before and after eating, to find your response.

What is a carbohydrate-to-insulin ratio? Can I use this to eat what I want?

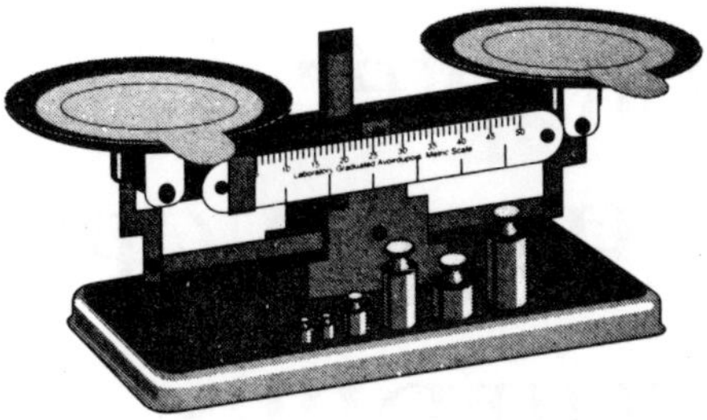

▼
TIP:

A carbohydrate-to-insulin ratio is used by people who manage diabetes with multiple daily injections or an insulin pump. The relationship between the food you eat and the insulin you take can be shown as a ratio—a carbohydrate-to-insulin ratio. This ratio tells you how much rapid-acting insulin to use, which is very useful when you eat more (or less) carbohydrate than usual. So, yes, you can eat unusual meals and determine the correct insulin dose. You have more flexibility in food choices and timing of meals. Take care, however, to choose foods that give you the nutrients you need and don't overindulge. To figure the insulin dose, you also take into account any exercise that you do.

Your carbohydrate-to-insulin ratio varies according to the meal or time of day. Many people have a lower carbohydrate-to-insulin ratio at breakfast than at dinner. The amount of fat, protein, and fiber in the meal will also affect the insulin's action. Blood glucose monitoring helps you adjust the ratio for different kinds of meals and mealtimes. Diabetes professionals can help you determine whether this approach will work for you.

Chapter 3 CHALLENGES OF CHILDREN

How often should my child have sweets?

▼
TIP:

Occasionally. Sweets are in the tiny top portion of the Diabetes Food Guide Pyramid, telling you to enjoy them when your nutrient needs from the other five groups have been met. If your child eats ice cream, cookies, and candy often or in large amounts, s/he won't have room for the foods s/he really needs. Some experts recommend offering sweets as part of a meal. This avoids making children think that sweets are special. Having sweets in appropriate amounts as part of the meal plan prevents the guilt feelings children may have about eating them. This approach also teaches that high-sugar foods are part of the carbohydrates in the meal plan, instead of an addition.

Many kid friendly foods may seem healthy, but the nutrient value is similar to candy or desserts. A fruit snack pouch is handy but may contain 100% sugar with only fruit flavoring. Look closely at labels to see how much of the carbohydrate content is sugar. A juicy piece of fresh fruit is also handy and supplies essential vitamins, minerals, and dietary fiber.

What do I do if my toddler refuses to eat his/her meal?

▼
TIP:

If you gave insulin before the meal, give your child a peanut butter and jelly sandwich or milk or a bigger portion of a food you know s/he will eat to cover the insulin given and prevent low blood glucose.

It is not uncommon for a toddler to refuse to eat. This can make parents anxious, especially if rapid- or short-acting insulin has already been given. Keep in mind that during the toddler stage, growth and appetite are slowing down, and your child is becoming an independent self-feeder. Your toddler may be eating adult table foods but is not ready for adult-size servings. Are you serving appropriate types and amounts of foods? Is your child joining the family in a regular schedule of meals and snacks? Be sure your child has enough time between meals and snacks so s/he will have an appetite. In some cases, you can give rapid-acting insulin after the meal and adjust the dose to the amount of food the child has eaten.

What if my child is napping, and it's time for a snack?

▼
TIP:

If your child's nap will pass snack time, you might test his/her blood glucose if your child is not startled and awakened by the finger-stick. Some children sleep through a stick. However, waking your child this way may be too traumatic. It may be better to simply wake your child and feed him/her.

For very young children, preventing low blood glucose is your goal. Low blood glucose levels are dangerous because they can affect the developing brain. Know your child's insulin types and doses and understand when they peak and how long they keep acting. You have to learn to balance the amount and type of insulin with food and eating times.

Discuss the following approaches to naptime snacks with your diabetes professionals:

- If your child's nap is 30 minutes to 1 hour after a meal, you don't need to test blood glucose or feed him/her before the nap.
- If your child's snack is scheduled for 3:00 P.M. and nap starts at 2:00 P.M., offer part of the snack before the nap and the rest after the nap.

Is it okay for my child to eat school lunches?

▼
TIP:

Probably. School lunches can fit into your child's meal plan, but you'll have to do some homework. Review menus with your child and select those that your child likes. Evaluate foods and serving sizes with your child's food and insulin plan in mind. Often, the cafeteria staff or your child must adjust the serving size. Food items may need to be added by the cafeteria or brought from home by your child, and some food items (sweetened fruit, fruit punch, or desserts) may need to be left off the tray.

Your child's comfort level with making changes in the menu, which may single him/her out as different, could cause a problem. Also, how willing are school personnel to work with you? A change in the menu may complicate things. Help your child learn how to choose basic foods. In junior high and high school, menu choices are more varied but may not be as healthy. Review nutrition information from fast food restaurants with your child to help him/her select foods that fit the meal plan. Carrying a lunch from home part of the time can help balance meals.

How do I handle trick-or-treating or other holiday activities for my child with diabetes?

TIP:

Part of growing up with diabetes is learning to make decisions about eating in special situations. Deciding *with your child* when, what kind, and how much candy s/he will eat can help form positive attitudes and feelings. If you talk with your child, you may find that food or treats are not what is most important to him/her about holiday activities.

Read the Nutrition Facts label on candy with your child and discuss the nutritional value of candy. Help your child make adjustments to the meal plan to include favorite treats from time to time. Some Halloween candy can be put in the freezer for later, if your child is not tempted by having it in the house. Discuss monitoring blood glucose carefully. Ask your diabetes team to explain the option of adjusting insulin upward to cover extra treats. Other family members can help by offering to trade some of the child's candy for money, movie passes, sleepovers, staying up late, or use of a big brother or sister's stereo. Plan ahead to prevent frustration and disappointment.

I have type 1 diabetes. Will I be able to breastfeed?

TIP:

Yes, you and your baby can enjoy all the benefits of breastfeeding. Enroll in a prenatal program for women with diabetes. Develop a breastfeeding meal plan and blood glucose goals with an RD. Breastfeeding lowers blood glucose and requires an extra 500 calories a day, but your insulin needs will drop to about half of what you used during pregnancy. You must monitor blood glucose carefully to adjust your insulin to your new eating and sleeping patterns and your infant's demands for milk. Checking blood glucose right before breastfeeding is wise. To avoid low blood glucose, eat a snack such as a glass of milk, piece of fruit, or a few crackers before or during breastfeeding and before taking a nap. A meal 1–2 hours before nursing works as well. Discuss all this with your diabetes team.

High blood glucose levels may lead to breast infections (mastitis). To prevent infection, alternate breasts when feeding; clean the breasts with water after feedings and let them air dry; learn proper infant latching-on techniques; drink plenty of water; and avoid wearing tight bras.

Chapter 4
THE SKINNY ON FAT

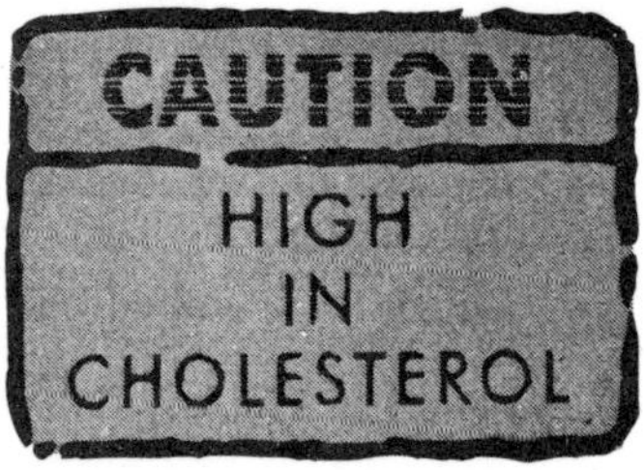

What should my cholesterol level be? What is the difference between "good" and "bad" cholesterol?

TIP:

The target for total cholesterol in adults is less than 200 mg/dl. For children and adolescents, it is less than 170 mg/dl.

ADA recommends that people with diabetes have blood lipids checked every year. A lipid profile measures the levels of high-density lipoprotein (HDL), low-density lipoprotein (LDL), and triglycerides. HDL (good) cholesterol carries cholesterol from every part of the body back to the liver for disposal. If you have high levels of HDL cholesterol (higher than 45 mg/dl), you are less likely to have heart disease. LDL (bad) cholesterol carries cholesterol from the liver to other tissues. Along the way, it forms deposits on the walls of arteries and other blood vessels. High levels of LDL cholesterol (above 130 mg/dl) show an increased risk of heart disease. Your body stores extra fat and calories as triglycerides. Good triglyceride levels are less than 200 mg/dl.

Blood Lipid Goals for People with Diabetes*	
Total Cholesterol	<200 mg/dl
LDL (bad) Cholesterol	<100 mg/dl
HDL (good) Cholesterol	>45 mg/dl
Triglycerides	<200 mg/dl

*1999 American Diabetes Association Clinical Practice Recommendations

How much can changes in diet lower my blood cholesterol level?

TIP:

Diet changes may decrease your LDL (bad) cholesterol by 15–25 mg/dl. For every 1% decrease in your total cholesterol, you decrease your risk for heart disease by 2%. Wouldn't you rather improve your risk factors for heart disease without medications, using diet changes only?

A heart-healthy eating plan is low in saturated fat and dietary cholesterol with total fat around 30% of total calories. This helps reduce blood cholesterol. Eating foods containing more fiber, such as oatmeal, can also help reduce blood levels of cholesterol (see p. 14). An RD can help you find the best amount of fat, carbohydrate, and protein in your food choices to lower your cholesterol, maintain healthy weight, and have good blood glucose control.

The following suggestions can help you eat low-fat meals:

- Select lean meats and cook with little or no fat
- Choose low-fat or fat-free milk products
- Eat less meat, cheese, and bacon
- Eat low-fat breads and starchy foods, such as potatoes, rice, and beans
- Remember that sweets are often also high in fat

Is it more important to decrease the cholesterol or the saturated fat in my diet?

TIP:

Focus on the saturated fat. Decreasing saturated fat in your diet has a more significant effect on your blood cholesterol level. Saturated fats come mainly from animal foods, such as meat, poultry, butter, and whole milk, and from coconut, palm, and palm kernel oils. Foods high in saturated fats are firm at room temperature.

To eat less saturated fat, use liquid vegetable oils instead of shortening, margarine, or butter whenever you can. Cut back on total fat and you'll likely reduce saturated fats, too. Check for saturated fat on Nutrition Facts panels on food labels. Check the ingredient list also. A food labeled "low in saturated fat" must contain one gram or less saturated fat per serving and no more than 15% of calories from saturated fat.

Your liver makes most of the cholesterol in your body, but every cell can also make cholesterol. When the body makes too much, the risk for heart disease goes up. Cholesterol also comes from animal foods. Cholesterol is found in milk, meat, poultry, eggs, fish, and dairy foods. However, dietary cholesterol doesn't automatically become blood cholesterol.

How can I boost good (HDL) cholesterol and lower bad (LDL) cholesterol?

TIP:

To increase HDL cholesterol and lower LDL cholesterol

- Stay physically active. It keeps HDL levels normal, reduces blood pressure, helps control stress, helps control body weight, gives your heart muscle a good workout, and improves blood glucose control.
- Lose weight.
- Reduce the fat in your diet to no more than 30% of calories from fat, and 10% from saturated fat. Replace some saturated fat in your diet with monounsaturated fats.
- Stop smoking. Smoking may lower HDL cholesterol levels and is a key factor in sudden death from cardiovascular disease. Smoking seems to raise blood pressure and heart rate and may increase the tendency of blood to clot and lead to a heart attack.

Other ways to decrease your LDL cholesterol are to

- Improve blood glucose control. It may decrease LDL cholesterol by up to 10–15%.
- Eat high-fiber foods, such as beans, oatmeal, oat bran, wheat bran, barley, and some fruits and vegetables. They contain soluble fiber, which seems to lower LDL cholesterol levels.

How do I know if I'm eating the right amount of fat?

TIP:

Talk to an RD about the right amount of fat for you, based on your weight and blood glucose and lipid goals. Most people eat too much fat. Fats contain 9 calories per gram, which means they contain a lot of calories in a small amount of food.

Write down what you eat for a few days, including the fat grams in your foods. The Nutrition Facts panel on food labels gives this information. For most people, fat should contribute about 30% of total calories for the day. Here is how to figure the number of grams of fat to eat if 30% of your 1,800 calories come from fat:

To find 30% of 1,800 calories,

$1{,}800 \times 0.30 = 540$ calories from fat

To find the number of fat grams in 540 calories

(9 calories per 1 gram of fat)

$540 \div 9 = 60$ grams of fat per day

Total Calories	Fat (g) for 30% of Calories
1200	40
1500	50
1800	60
2100	70
2400	80
2600	87

Can I have an unlimited amount of fat-free foods?

▼

TIP:

No. Fat free does not mean the food is calorie free or carbohydrate free. Nor does it mean that it is a "free food." A free food is a term used by people with diabetes for foods that have less than 20 calories or less than 5 grams of carbohydrate per serving.

Fat-free foods have fat taken out and sometimes replaced by fat replacers. Some fat replacers, such as those used in fat-free salad dressings, contain carbohydrate and can affect your blood glucose level. Also, many fat-free foods have more sugar added to them for taste, and this will affect your blood glucose level.

If your weight and blood lipids are in a healthy range, you don't need fat-free foods. If your goal is to lower blood lipids and lose weight, moderate portions of some fat-free foods may help you. Read the Nutrition Facts on food labels to get the serving size, calories, and carbohydrate content to help you decide how fat-free foods fit into your meal plan.

How can I eat more monounsaturated fats?

▼
TIP:

Use olive oil, canola oil, or nuts in your meals. ADA recommends that you replace part of your dietary fat, especially saturated fat, with monounsaturated fats. Keep in mind, these healthier fats must *replace* saturated or polyunsaturated fat in the diet rather than be added to it. In other words, don't increase the total fat content of your meal plan.

Nuts can substitute for animal protein in recipes or be eaten in small servings as snacks. Garnish vegetables with slivered almonds, hazelnuts, or pine nuts instead of butter. Use nut butters (such as peanut, cashew, or almond butter) without partially hydrogenated oils. Avocados can be sliced and added to a sandwich of tomato, sprouts, or other vegetables.

Prepare salad dressings or pastas with olive oil. Cook (sauté, stir-fry, or broil) with small amounts of olive or canola oil. Canola oil is a monounsaturated fat that is less expensive than olive oil and lighter in taste. When you substitute a liquid oil for a solid shortening in a recipe, use 1/4 less oil.

What are trans fatty acids and how do they affect my diabetes?

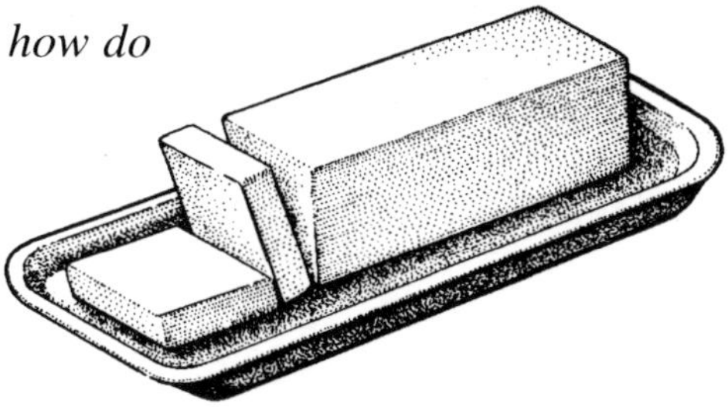

TIP:

Trans fatty acids are formed in processed foods during hydrogenation. Hydrogenation makes a fat solid when it is at room temperature. For example, liquid vegetable oil is partially hydrogenated to make stick margarine. Partially hydrogenated vegetable oil is used in fried foods, baked products, and snack foods.

Trans fatty acids don't affect blood glucose levels but do increase blood cholesterol levels, which increases your risk for heart disease. If less than 30% of your calories come from fat and 10% from saturated fat, you're probably okay. If you eat a moderately high-fat diet, your trans fatty acid intake may be too high. Don't eat many processed foods. Choose soft table spreads instead of stick margarine. Read food labels and select margarine that contains no more than 2 grams of saturated fat per tablespoon and liquid oil as the first ingredient. Look for baked products, convenience dinners, and snack foods with less than 2 grams of saturated fat per serving. Use vegetable oil instead of solid shortening in cooking. Check with your RD if you have questions about trans fatty acids.

Does it matter what kind of margarine and vegetable oil I use?

▼
TIP:

It depends on the fatty acids they contain—saturated, polyunsaturated, and monounsaturated. Saturated fats (butter and lard) are the least healthy. Polyunsaturated fats (corn or soybean oil) are healthier. Monounsaturated fats (canola or olive oil) are the best. All fats are actually mixtures of these three fatty acids.

All margarines are made of vegetable oil. However, the fat is hydrogenated (saturated), so it is less healthy than oil. Tub and squeeze margarines also contain water and air to lower fat and calories. Read the food label to find margarine with only 2 grams of saturated fat per serving and liquid oil as the first ingredient.

Canola and olive oil are the best vegetable oils because they are low in saturated fat and have the largest amount of monounsaturated fats. Safflower, sunflower, corn, and soybean oil are also low in saturated fat.

Hint: If you want the taste of butter but not all the saturated fat, whip 1 cup of canola oil into 1 cup of butter!

What are fat replacers, and how do they affect my diabetes?

▼
TIP:

Fat replacers are used to give reduced-calorie foods the texture, appearance, and taste of full-fat products. Most fat replacers are made from carbohydrates and can raise your blood glucose level. The ones made of protein or fat are not so likely to affect blood glucose. Remember that food with a fat replacer can still have lots of calories.

Fat replacers made from carbohydrates include polydextrose, cellulose gum, corn syrup solids, dextrin, maltodextrin, hydrogenated starch hydrolysate, carrageenan and modified food starch. They combine with water to provide thicker texture, as in fat-free salad dressings. Fat replacers made from protein include Simplesse™ and whey protein concentrate. They are used in cheese, sour cream, salad dressings, baked goods, butter, and mayonnaise spreads.

Olestra™ is a fat replacer found in salty snacks. Made from sugar and fat, it does not act like fat. It is not digested, so it contributes no calories. It may cause cramping, diarrhea, and inhibit the absorption of some fat-soluble vitamins.

Check the Nutrition Facts panel for calories and the amount of carbohydrate, fat, and protein in foods with fat replacers. Ask your RD to help you work these foods into your meal plan.

Chapter 5
HOW SWEET IT IS

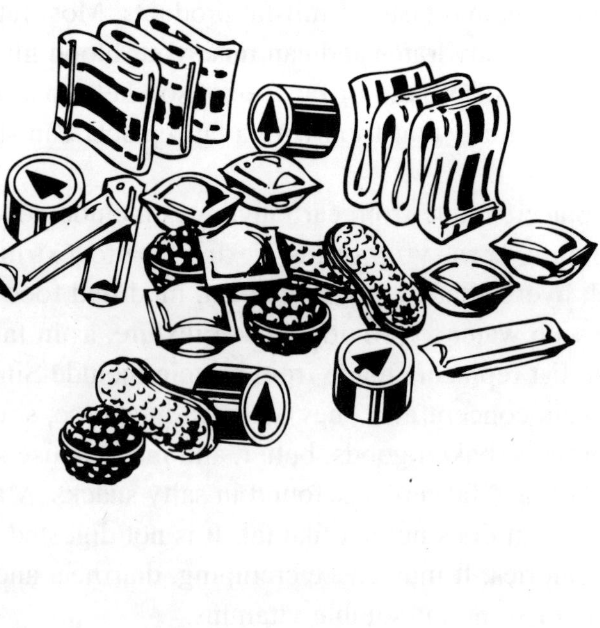

Does eating sugar cause diabetes?

TIP:

No. Although diabetes has been called "sugar diabetes" for many years, eating sugar does not cause it. Type 1 diabetes happens when your body's immune system destroys the insulin-producing beta cells in the pancreas. Factors that may cause the immune system to do this are autoantibodies, cow's milk (see p. 107), genes, and oxygen-free radicals (see p. 80). Type 1 diabetes is probably triggered by one of these environmental factors in people who have the genes for developing the disease.

Type 2 diabetes is different from type 1. The bodies of most people with type 2 make insulin but can't use it well. Genetics plays a strong role in type 2 diabetes, as does age, obesity, and lifestyle. Obese individuals who eat a high-calorie diet and don't participate in physical activity are more likely to develop type 2 diabetes. In this case, too much sugar may provide excess calories, in the same way excess fat does. The resulting weight gain and obesity, which interfere with the action of insulin, can lead to the development of type 2 diabetes.

I'm confused about sugars and starches. Will a brownie or a piece of bread raise my blood glucose the most?

▼
TIP:

Sugars and starches are carbohydrates and, eaten in equal amounts, they raise blood glucose the same. A small brownie (15 grams of carbohydrate) raises blood glucose the same as one slice of bread (15 grams of carbohydrate).

For years, we thought that the body absorbed sugar more quickly than starch, and people were told to avoid sweets. Research has shown that sugar is okay for people with diabetes if it is part of a meal plan. It is substituted for other carbohydrate foods. Focus on the total amount of carbohydrate that you eat rather than on whether it comes from starch or sugar.

Certain factors affect the way your blood glucose responds to sugars and starches. When you eat sweets, observe whether other foods are eaten at the same time, how quickly you eat, how the food was prepared, and the amount of protein and fat in the food. Measure your blood glucose 1–2 hours after eating and note the affect sugar has on it. Use this information to make decisions about including sweets in your meal plan.

How many grams of sugar am I allowed to eat in a day?

▼

TIP:

There is no magic number of grams for each day, but eat sugar sparingly. Sugar has calories but few vitamins or minerals. Foods high in sugar are usually high in fat, which can lead to poor diabetes control and weight gain.

The Nutrition Facts label gives the number of grams of sugar in the food. This number includes both natural and added sugars. Natural sugars are found naturally in foods, such as fructose in raisins or lactose in milk. These sugars provide some vitamins and minerals. Added sugars are put into foods to make them sweet, such as sugar in cookies or high fructose corn syrup in soft drinks. These sugars provide calories but no other nutrients.

When you read the food label, check the type of sugar the food contains, but focus on the grams of total carbohydrate rather than the grams of sugar. Sugar and sweets are fine occasionally, in small portions, if you substitute them for other carbohydrate foods in your meal plan and check your blood glucose to see how the food affects you.

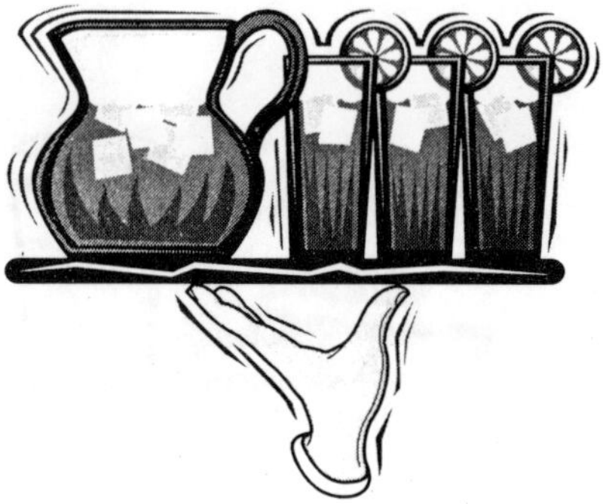

Are there sweeteners that are free foods? How can I tell which to use?

TIP:

Yes. "Nonnutritive" sweeteners are free foods because they have no calories or carbohydrate. They don't raise blood glucose levels. None of them are perfect for all uses. Some are great in cold beverages but won't work in baked goods. While the sweeteners themselves are calorie free, don't forget to count the calories, fat, and carbohydrate in the foods they are sweetening.

Sweetener	Calories (per gram)	Other Names	Description
Saccharin	0	Sweet 'n Low	200–700 times sweeter than sucrose; suitable for cooking and baking
Aspartame	0	Nutrasweet, Equal	160–220 times sweeter than sucrose; may change flavor if heated
Acesulfame-K	0	Sunette, Sweet One	200 times sweeter than sucrose; suitable for cooking and baking
Sucralose	0	Splenda	600 times sweeter than sucrose; suitable for cooking and baking

What calorie-containing sweeteners can I use instead of sugar?

▼
TIP:

Sugar and all the other calorie-containing sweeteners provide about the same amount of calories and raise your blood glucose in the same way. Fructose, honey, and other "natural" sweeteners have no advantages over the other sweeteners that contain calories. You can substitute the nutritive sweeteners listed below for other carbohydrates in your meal plan. Remember to count the calories and carbohydrate they contain.

Sweetener	Calories (per gram)	Other Names	Description
Sucrose	4	granulated sugar, table sugar, powdered sugar, brown sugar, molasses	sweetens; enhances flavor, texture, and appearance of baked goods
Fructose	4	fruit sugar, high fructose corn syrup	sweetens; functions like sucrose in baking; may produce a lower rise in blood glucose than sucrose; in large amounts raises LDL (bad) cholesterol
Sugar alcohols	2–3	sorbitol, mannitol, xylitol, isomalt, lactitol, malitol, hydrogenated starch hydrolysate	25–90% as sweet as sucrose; may produce laxative effect in large doses

Can I eat all I want of food that is labeled "sugar free"?

TIP:

No. A food labeled sugar free must contain less than 0.5 grams of sugar per serving, but it may have calories and carbohydrate. For example, sugar-free pudding has 0 grams of sugar, but it also has 70 calories and 6 grams of carbohydrate in a 1/2-cup serving. If you were to eat unlimited amounts, you could easily add enough calories and carbohydrate to sabotage your diabetes and weight-control efforts over time.

Although the sweetener used in a sugar-free product may be calorie free (such as acesulfame potassium, aspartame, saccharin, or sucralose), the other ingredients in the food usually contain fat, carbohydrate, protein, and calories. Nonnutritive sweeteners may be used along with other sweeteners that contain calories, so don't rely on the "sugar-free" symbol on the front of the package alone. Read the ingredient list and food label carefully so you can make the best choices for healthy eating (see p. 8).

What are sugar alcohols? Will foods with sugar alcohols cause my blood glucose to rise?

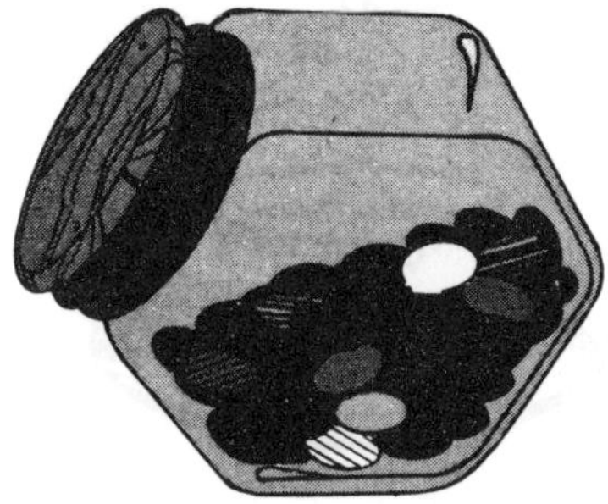

▼
TIP:

Sugar alcohols (also known as polyols) are used to sweeten a variety of foods, such as candy, chewing gum, baked goods, ice cream, and fruit spreads. They are also found in toothpaste, mouthwash, and medications, including cough syrups and throat lozenges. Sugar alcohols have 2–3 calories per gram, compared to 4 calories per gram in other sugars. Sugar alcohols are absorbed more slowly than other sugars and cause a smaller rise in blood glucose levels after they are eaten.

Because sugar alcohols are not completely digested in the stomach, you may experience side effects such as diarrhea, intestinal cramping, or gas if you eat too much of them. One recommendation is to eat no more than 20–50 grams of sugar alcohol in a day, which is the amount found in 12–33 pieces of sugar alcohol–sweetened hard candy.

The sugar alcohols you'll see on food labels include:

Hydrogenated starch hydrolysate
Isomalt
Lactitol
Mannitol
Malitol
Sorbitol
Xylitol

What is stevia?

▼
TIP:

Stevia is a sweetener 30–300 times sweeter than sugar, but it has no calories. It is made from an herb and comes in three forms. The greenish-black liquid is 70 times sweeter than sugar and is used to sweeten cereal, tea, coffee, and hot chocolate. It's also used in baking but may change the color of foods. The crushed leaf form is 30 times as sweet as sugar. It comes in small tea-bag packets and is sprinkled on cereal and other foods. The leaf particles do not dissolve. The third form of stevia is a white, heat-stable powder that is 300 times sweeter than sugar. The liquid and leaf forms have a slight taste of anise (licorice).

Although it is used in Brazil and Japan, stevia has not been approved as a food additive by the Food and Drug Administration (FDA) here. However, health food stores sell it for personal use. There is no research available describing the effects of stevia when used by a person with diabetes. Side effects are also unknown, so discuss the product with your health care team and use caution until more information is available.

Chapter 6
FOOD AND FITNESS

What kind of exercise burns off enough calories to lose weight?

▼
TIP:

To lose a pound of body weight you need to burn 3,500 calories—not all at once, but over several days. Most people lose weight by getting more exercise each day and cutting back their food by about 500 calories a day.

The more frequently and more intensely you exercise, the more calories you burn. And exercise includes everyday activities such as vacuuming and gardening. If you are moderately active every day, you will burn about 150 calories, or about 1,000 calories a week. With exercise alone and no diet changes, you would lose 1 pound in 3–4 weeks. A combination of exercise and chores gives you variety.

Activity	**Body Weight**	
(30 minutes)	**120 lbs**	**170 lbs**
Aerobic dance	165 calories	230 calories
Bicycling	110	155
Bowling	85	115
Gardening	140	195
Golf (walking)	125	175
Hiking	165	230
Housework	70	95
Mowing lawn	150	215
Swimming, leisurely	165	230
Tennis	195	270
Walking, brisk	110	155

Do I need a snack when I exercise?

▼
TIP:

If you take insulin or oral diabetes medication, it will depend on your blood glucose level. Check before and after exercise and during long, hard exercise. (If blood glucose is more than 250 mg/dl, do not exercise until it is under control.)

- **30 minutes of low intensity exercise** (walking): If blood glucose is less than 100 mg/dl before exercise, eat a snack with 15 grams of carbohydrate.
- **30–60 minutes of moderate intensity exercise** (tennis, swimming, jogging): If blood glucose is less than 100 mg/dl before exercise, have a snack with 25–50 grams of carbohydrate. If blood glucose is 100–180 mg/dl, eat 10–15 grams of carbohydrate.
- **1–2 hours of strenuous intensity exercise** (basketball, skiing, shoveling snow): If blood glucose is less than 100 mg/dl before exercise, add a snack with about 50 grams of carbohydrate. If blood glucose is 100–180 mg/dl, add a snack with 25–50 grams of carbohydrate. If blood glucose is 180–250 mg/dl, have a snack with 10–15 grams of carbohydrate. At this intense level of exercise, always monitor blood glucose carefully.

What are some foods or beverages to use with exercise?

▼
TIP:

If you take insulin or oral diabetes medicine, you may need a snack before, during, or after you exercise. Muscles keep burning glucose even after you stop exercising. It may take the body up to 24 hours to replace glucose stores used during exercise. After strenuous exercise, you may need to monitor your blood glucose every 1–2 hours (see p. 61).

When you are exercising, don't wait to be thirsty to drink plenty of fluid. Dehydration can hinder your strength and endurance. Cool water is absorbed faster than warm water. Diluted fruit juice or sports drinks provide carbohydrate and fluids for exercise that lasts more than 1 hour.

Food for Exercise
(15 g carbohydrate)

- 1 small piece fresh fruit
- 2 Tbsp raisins
- 3 graham crackers
- 1/2 English muffin or bagel
- 1 small muffin
- 6–8 oz sports drink
- 1 cup yogurt
- 4–5 snack crackers
- 1/4 cup dried fruit
- 1/2 cup fruit juice (can be diluted)

Can I use sports drinks when I exercise?

▼
TIP:

Water is the best drink when you're exercising less than 1 hour. Every human needs carbohydrate during exercise that lasts more than 1 hour and is moderate to high intensity (swimming, jogging, soccer, shoveling heavy snow). When muscle stores of fuel are used up, blood glucose supplies the fuel for prolonged exercise. Sports drinks provide fluids, are easy to take, and are easier to digest than food during prolonged exercise. Certain sports drinks are better than others. Drinks with a concentration of carbohydrate or sugars greater than 10% (such as fruit juice and regular soda) may not be absorbed well and cause cramps, nausea, diarrhea, or bloating. Diluted fruit juice (1/2 water, 1/2 juice) works better.

	Portion Size	Calories (g)	Carbo-hydrate	Carbohydrate Concen-tration (%)
All Sport Body Quencher	8 oz	70	20	8
Exceed Energy Drink Powder	2 Tbsp + 8 oz water	70	17	7
Gatorade Thirst Quencher	8 oz	50	14	6
Power Ade Thirst Quencher	8 oz	70	19	8

When should I eat breakfast and take my insulin if I work out early in the morning?

▼
TIP:

To exercise before breakfast: First check your blood glucose. If it is 100 mg/dl or higher, eat or drink 10–15 grams of carbohydrate, then exercise. If it is lower than 100 mg/dl, add another 10–15 grams of carbohydrate (total of 20–30 grams) and wait 10–15 minutes. Test again and if it is above 100 mg/dl, go exercise. You may need more carbohydrate during exercise, depending on the type of exercise. After exercise, check blood glucose again, take your insulin, and eat breakfast. You may need to decrease your usual morning dose of insulin, depending on the time and intensity of exercise.

To exercise after breakfast: If you work out 1–2 hours after breakfast, eat your usual breakfast. You may need more carbohydrate at breakfast or to adjust your insulin, but you need to keep a record of your blood glucose levels before, during, and after exercise to learn your response to exercise at particular times of the day. This helps you decide whether food and insulin adjustments are needed.

I'm 65. Can I start a weight-training program now? Do I need an amino acid (protein supplement)?

▼
TIP:

Weight (or resistance) training can give you more strength and endurance for your daily activities and help prevent osteoporosis. Building muscle mass is not just for young people. As you get older, your body loses muscle mass and tone unless you do something about it. You want muscle mass because muscles burn calories even when you are doing absolutely nothing. So the benefits of weight training go way beyond those you see in the mirror.

If you get serious about weight training, your protein needs are only slightly higher (about 2–4 oz more meat, chicken, or fish a day). Excess protein can actually be harmful by causing dehydration and strain on the kidneys. You can get enough amino acids—and all the other essential nutrients that supplements don't supply—from the food you eat. Food also costs less than protein in powder or pill form.

Chapter 7
WEIGHTY ISSUES

What is BMI and why is it important?

TIP:

Body mass index, or BMI, combines your weight and height into one number. BMI applies to both men and women and is related to total body fat. The risk for type 2 diabetes, high blood pressure, lipid disorders, cardiovascular disease, gallbladder disease, osteoarthritis, sleep apnea, respiratory problems, and cancer rises in people whose BMI is over 25.

To find your BMI

1. Multiply your weight in pounds by 705
2. Divide your answer by your height in inches
3. Divide this answer by your height again

For example, a 5'6", 185-pound individual has a BMI of about 30.

Recent guidelines define overweight as a BMI of 25–29.9 and obesity as a BMI of 30 and above. Keep in mind that the BMI is only a guideline. A very muscular, active person could have a high BMI without health risks. On the other hand, a couch potato may have a lower BMI, yet have too much body fat.

If you are overweight or obese, the good news is that losing just 10% of your body weight will bring significant improvements in your health and diabetes control!

How can I determine my ideal body weight?

▼
TIP:

There is actually a range of body weights associated with good health. For example, a 5'5" man or woman should weigh between 114 and 150 pounds. You must consider your age, gender, body shape, and location of body fat. Talk to your health care providers about the best weight for you.

People with fat around the upper body, waist, and abdomen ("apple" shape) tend to have more health problems than those who put on fat on the lower body, hips, and thighs ("pear" shape). Health problems associated with apple shapes include insulin resistance, higher blood cholesterol, tendency toward heart and blood vessel disease, and high blood pressure.

To determine your body shape (waist-to-hip ratio):

1. Measure around waist or 1 inch above navel
2. Measure hips at biggest point
3. Divide waist measurement by hip measurement

For a woman, a ratio of greater than 0.8 means an apple shape; a ratio of less than 0.8 means a pear. For a man, a ratio greater than 1.0 means an apple, and a ratio of less than 1.0 means a pear.

I need to lose weight to improve my blood glucose levels, but I can't get started. How can I set a reasonable weight loss goal and achieve it?

▼
TIP:

Setting realistic goals is the key. If you start with a modest weight loss goal of 10–15 pounds, you are more likely to achieve and maintain it. (A weight loss of as little as 10–15% of your weight can lower your health risks.) Once you've reached your first goal, you can assess your progress, and set your sights on the next target.

When you have chosen a weight-loss goal, these tips can help you get started.

- Write down your goal and keep it where you can be reminded of it each day.
- Share your goal with someone who will see your progress, such as your health care team or a caring friend.
- Take one immediate action to get started. For example, schedule an appointment with an RD or join an exercise class. Taking action improves your chances for success!
- Commit to small daily actions, such as packing a healthy lunch rather than going out for fast food.
- Find new ways to deal with stress, such as taking a walk or doing yoga.

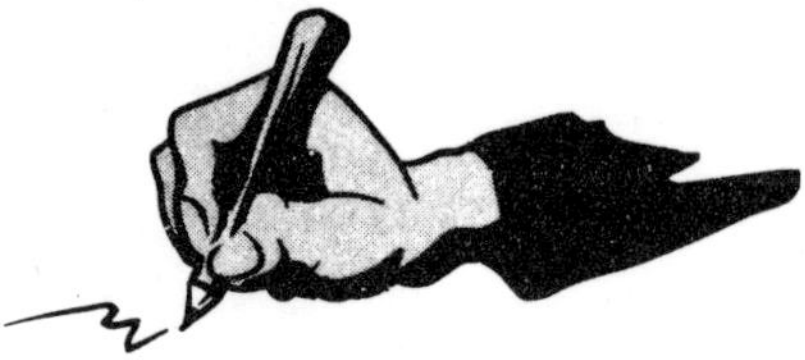

Why can some people maintain their weight loss, while others regain every pound?

▼
TIP:

Researchers have found that people who maintain their weight loss have done certain things to succeed. You can try the following:

- Get help in developing a personalized meal plan that works for you, rather than following a preprinted diet from a magazine or book.
- Exercise. Increased physical activity is one of the best ways to keep lost weight from returning.
- Keep records of blood glucose levels, physical activity, and the food you eat.
- Surround yourself with friends or relatives who support your efforts. They help you keep going!
- Stay away from a quick-fix approach and commit to long-term weight control.
- Don't deny yourself. Occasionally eat small portions of your favorite foods.
- Find other ways to cope with everyday problems instead of smoking, sleeping, drinking, or eating too much.
- Do your best, but don't make excuses, pity yourself, or put yourself down if you aren't perfect in your efforts.
- Be upbeat. Believe that you will succeed and attempt to make your life happier and more fulfilling.

Help! My diet isn't working any more. What am I doing wrong?

▼
TIP:

It may not be your diet. Diabetes and its treatments can affect how you lose weight. People who achieve tight glucose control may gain weight because they start absorbing all the energy from their food, rather than losing calories through urine (see p. 28). Improvement in your diabetes control is the best measure of health success, rather than the numbers on your scale. Ask yourself:

- Do I have the wrong goal? Your goal is not a certain weight but improved diabetes control. Don't step on the scale too often.
- Can I increase my physical activity? Look for ways to add activity every day—walking more, using stairs instead of elevators.
- Am I snacking on too many fat-free foods? Fat free doesn't mean calorie free. Fruit, cut-up vegetables, and whole grains are better snacks.
- Am I eating a variety of foods? A rigid weight-loss plan may keep you from learning how to add variety to your meals. Diet boredom can lead to overeating.
- How are my serving sizes? Too much of a good thing can make a difference in weight and diabetes management (see p. 7).

I'm having a hard time sticking with my weight-loss plan. Are there any quick tips to keep me on the right track?

TIP:

Here are some tried and true tips:

- Keep weight-loss goals reasonable. You can't lose 25 pounds, stop smoking, AND begin walking 3 miles a day all in one week!
- Set small weight-loss targets. Aim for 5-pound goals.
- Record your weight and blood glucose levels. It's encouraging to see improvements in blood glucose, even if your weight doesn't change.
- Periodically, write down what you eat for one day. Measure your serving sizes.
- Drink a large glass of water before every meal.
- Use a smaller plate.
- Eat slowly and stop when you just begin to feel full.
- Put your fork down between mouthfuls and chew thoroughly.
- Keep low-calorie snacks on hand—sugar-free gelatin, cut-up fresh vegetables, and fresh fruit.
- Don't deprive yourself of your favorite food. Cut back on how often you eat it or on your serving size.
- Expect setbacks and don't give up. Begin again tomorrow.

Won't skipping meals help me cut back on calories and lose weight?

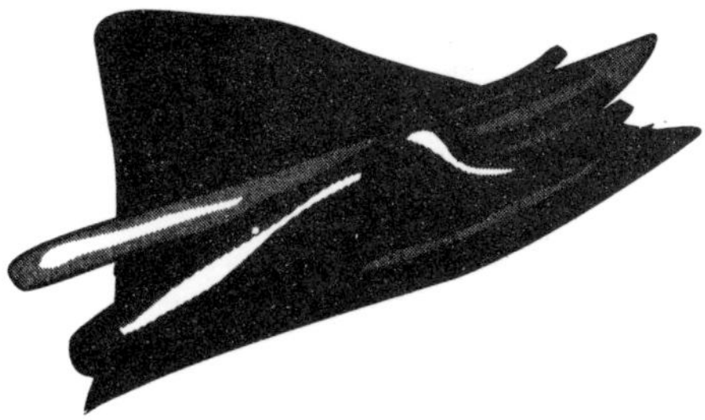

▼
TIP:

No. Eating all your calories in one or two big meals can send your blood glucose levels sky-high. Eating smaller meals more often keeps the amount of carbohydrate entering your system small and consistent, so your glucose level stays within your target range. This can keep your weight under control. And you'll need less insulin.

When to eat depends on many factors, particularly the type of diabetes medication you use. If you take insulin, skipping meals can result in dangerous hypoglycemia. Skipping meals can make you hungrier, moody, and unable to focus. This may lead to overeating later in the day. Breakfast-skippers are particularly at risk for grabbing sugary, high-fat foods later in the day (see p. 19). Always eat within a few hours of getting up.

Your metabolism slows down when you do not eat. Eating regularly keeps your energy level high and helps your body burn calories. Eating more often doesn't mean that you eat more calories. See an RD to learn to spread your calories throughout the day. You may find that three meals and three snacks work better for you!

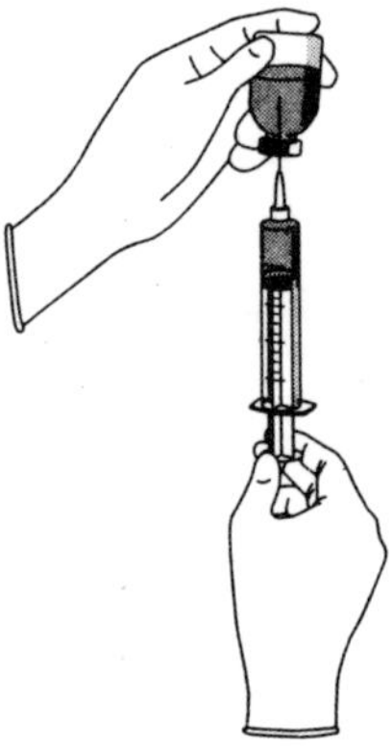

Won't skipping a few doses of insulin help me lose weight?

▼

TIP:

If you take too little insulin on purpose, your body will not use all the calories you eat, and this will result in weight loss. However, it is a very dangerous way to lose a few pounds. An inadequate dose of insulin means you will have higher blood glucose levels and poor diabetes control. This can affect growth and development in children and adolescents. In the short term, high blood glucose levels cause headache, blurred vision, and upset stomach and make you feel tired, hungry, and thirsty. Underdosing insulin puts you at greater risk for ketoacidosis and having to be hospitalized. It can be life-threatening.

Long-term diabetes complications such as nerve damage, kidney damage, and diabetic eye disease are more likely to develop if you deliberately underdose insulin to control your weight. Some researchers have found that people who misuse insulin have a high rate of psychological problems and may have more difficulty dealing with the diagnosis of diabetes.

Don't skip your insulin shot. Stick to a sensible, health-promoting plan of eating and physical activity to lose weight!

Will a very-low-calorie diet work for me?

▼
TIP:

Probably not. They are for people with type 2 diabetes who are extremely obese and at immediate risk for serious health problems. Weight loss on a very-low-calorie diet (VLCD) is rapid, and blood glucose levels fall within a few days of beginning this restrictive way of eating. VLCDs are not for people with type 1 diabetes, because of the risk of hypoglycemia. A person with diabetes and kidney disease should not try VLCDs because of the high-protein content of the diet.

Most VLCDs are based on drinking a beverage or eating very lean meat. These diets are high in protein to prevent muscle tissue from wasting away and supplemented with vitamins and minerals because so little food is eaten. Because of the side effects, VLCDs should only be used under the supervision of a physician who specializes in the care of people with diabetes and obesity.

Unfortunately, a VLCD can be costly, and most people regain all the weight they lost within five years. It might jump-start a weight-loss effort, but for truly permanent weight loss, you must make lasting changes in your lifestyle.

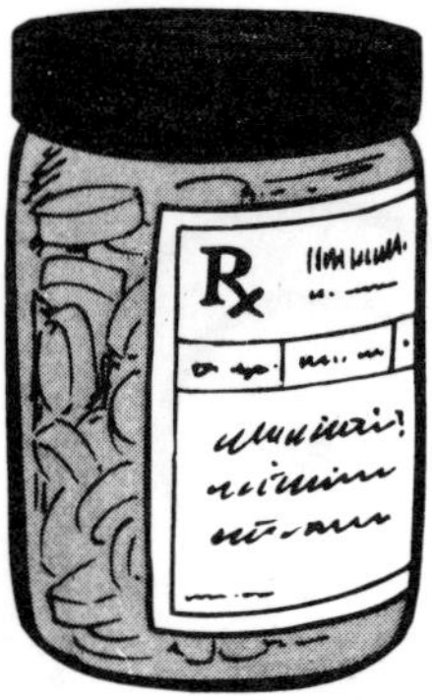

Why can't I just take diet pills to help me lose weight faster?

▼
TIP:

There is no "magic bullet." To lose weight you eat less or exercise more—or both. Diet pills are meant to be used along with meal planning and exercise, not in place of them. These pills have side effects and should not be taken without your health care provider's advice. Weight-loss medications are not for everyone and cannot be used long term.

Weight-loss drugs work by controlling your appetite, increasing your sense of fullness, or changing the absorption of the fat you eat. Pills that control appetite and feelings of fullness act on brain chemicals. They cause you to feel less hungry, making it easier to stick with a low-calorie diet. Side effects include dry mouth, insomnia, jitteriness, and increased heart rate and blood pressure.

Drugs that change fat absorption don't reduce appetite but prevent the absorption of about 30% of the calories from the fat you eat. The fat is lost in the stools, leading to side effects of oily or loose stools and intestinal gas.

What is leptin? When will it be available for people with type 2 diabetes?

▼
TIP:

Leptin is a hormone made in fat cells that may regulate food intake and body weight by telling the brain when the body contains enough fat. A study of 123 humans reported that daily injections of leptin, in combination with a reduced-calorie diet, led to significant weight loss (average of 16 pounds over 6 months for those on the highest doses). The most common side effects were redness and itching or swelling at the injection site—common when human proteins are injected.

None of the participants in the study had diabetes, but the data suggest that leptin had a beneficial effect on blood glucose levels. It is not clear whether the effect was due to the leptin or the weight loss, but both weight loss and improved blood glucose levels are beneficial for people with type 2 diabetes. The journey from research laboratory to drugstore shelf is often a long one (3–5 years). The next steps are more research studies and then approval from the FDA.

Chapter 8
OFF THE BEATEN TRACK

Should I take chromium supplements or can I get enough from foods?

▼ TIP:

If you eat a healthy diet, you are getting enough chromium. Ads claim that chromium supplements will help overcome obesity, help the body use insulin better, prevent hypoglycemia, and take away sugar cravings. The body needs chromium to metabolize protein, carbohydrate, and fat, and to produce glucose tolerance factor, which is believed to help insulin work better. The estimated safe and adequate daily dietary intake of chromium is 50–200 mcg per day for healthy adults—a tiny amount. Chromium is found in Brewer's yeast, wheat germ, corn oil, whole-grain cereals, meats, cheese, bran, liver, kidney, oysters, potatoes with the skin left on, peanuts, and peanut butter.

People who do not eat healthy foods and suffer from malnutrition, especially the elderly, may be at risk for chromium deficiency. Supplements are recommended only for people with signs and symptoms of a deficiency, which is difficult to detect. Let the buyer beware. Most chromium supplements contain more than chromium, are poorly absorbed, and are not regulated by the FDA. Chromium supplements can be expensive, using up money that might be better spent on healthy foods.

I've heard so much about antioxidants. Will taking them help my diabetes?

▼
TIP:

It may. Antioxidants include vitamins A, C, and E, beta-carotene, and the mineral selenium. They protect the body from harmful substances known as *free radicals*. Free radicals are by-products of metabolism that disrupt our natural cancer-fighting defenses and destroy important structures such as cell membranes and DNA. High blood glucose helps free radicals form in the body, and free radicals may be involved in diabetes complications.

Research shows that people who eat antioxidant-rich foods have less cancer and heart disease. However, we don't know whether it is because of the antioxidants or the food they're contained in. Your best bet is to eat a variety of foods rich in antioxidants. You find

- Beta-carotene and vitamin A in green leafy vegetables (broccoli, collard greens, kale, spinach) and red, orange, and yellow fruits and vegetables (apricot, cantaloupe, carrots, mango, peach, pumpkin, sweet potato, tomato, watermelon, squash)
- Vitamin C in broccoli, cantaloupe, citrus fruit (orange, grapefruit, lemon), kiwi, potato, red pepper, strawberries, tomato
- Vitamin E in almonds, nuts, seeds, vegetable oil, wheat germ
- Selenium in cashews, halibut, meat, oysters, salmon, scallops, tuna

Will a magnesium supplement improve my diabetes control?

▼
TIP:

Only if you are magnesium deficient. Magnesium deficiency may play a role in causing insulin resistance, carbohydrate intolerance, and hypertension. But only people at risk for a magnesium deficiency should have a blood test for magnesium levels. People at risk are those with congestive heart failure, potassium or calcium deficiency, or who are pregnant. Others at risk have had heart attacks, ketoacidosis, long-term feeding through the veins, long-term alcohol abuse, or have taken drugs such as diuretics for long periods of time. Symptoms of magnesium deficiency might include irregular heartbeat, nausea, weakness, and mental derangement.

Magnesium is found in all kinds of foods. The best sources are legumes, nuts, whole grains, and green vegetables. The RDA for adult males is 350 mg a day; for females, it is 280 mg daily.

If a blood test shows that you are low in magnesium, your doctor will prescribe a supplement. People with kidney disease should only take a magnesium supplement under a doctor's care.

Food (serving)	Magnesium (mg)
spinach, boiled (1/2 cup)	80
peanut butter (2 Tbsp)	50
black-eyed peas (1/2 cup)	45
whole-wheat bread (1 slice)	25

Can vanadium (vanadyl sulfate) supplements improve my blood glucose levels?

▼
TIP:

We don't know. At this time there is not enough information to say. This trace element is being studied for its effect on insulin sensitivity and glucose-lowering ability in people with diabetes.

Vanadyl sulfate is marketed in health food stores as a supplement that "mimics the effect of insulin in the body, thereby lowering blood glucose levels." Some ads say that it "enables some people to use less insulin, or stop taking insulin altogether." Because supplements are not regulated in the same way as drugs in the United States, this type of claim is legal. But little is known about this supplement, and the side effects are unclear. Before taking it or adjusting your diabetes medications, talk with your diabetes professionals.

Recommended levels of vanadium have not been determined. If research proves a connection to blood glucose control and insulin action, vanadium would likely be regulated as a drug rather than a supplement.

What is fenugreek? Can it lower blood glucose and cholesterol?

▼ **TIP:**

Fenugreek is a plant used since ancient times for managing diabetes and obesity. Its seed is a spice found in Indian, Middle Eastern, and Mediterranean dishes. Fenugreek contains concentrated amounts of soluble and insoluble fiber and can lower blood cholesterol and slow the rise in blood glucose after eating. It is on the *Generally Recognized as Safe Food and Spice List* from the FDA.

A form of fenugreek is marketed under the name Limitrol in capsule, wafer, or pudding form. The manufacturer's data from unpublished research show the product diminishes the rise in blood glucose levels after eating by about 40%. They also claim that when the product was taken daily before the two largest meals, it reduced the average total blood cholesterol by 20% and LDL cholesterol by 26% after six weeks. Side effects are common to dietary fiber—excess gas, diarrhea, and poor absorption of glucose and fats.

The jury is still out. The manufacturer's studies have not been published in a medical journal nor have the health claims been evaluated by the FDA. Speak with your health care providers about fenugreek as a suitable product for you.

I've heard that folate will reduce my risk of heart attack. Do I need to take a folate supplement every day?

▼
TIP:

Because people with diabetes are at risk for heart and blood vessel disease, it may be wise for you to pay attention to the amount of folate in your diet. For several years, scientists have known that a daily 400-mcg supplement of the B-vitamin folate helps prevent certain birth defects when the mother takes it before conception. More recently, research has shown that 400 mcg of folate may reduce the risk of heart attacks by lowering elevated levels of homocysteine in the blood. Homocysteine is an amino acid that in excess amounts is toxic to blood vessels.

Ask your provider and RD whether they recommend a folate supplement for you. If you are interested in increasing the amount of folate you eat, the following list has some of the best food sources:

Food (serving)	Folate (mcg)
Spinach (1/2 cup)	130
Cooked navy beans (1/2 cup)	125
Wheat germ (1/4 cup)	80
Avocado (1/2)	55
Orange (1 medium)	45
Bread (1 slice, fortified)	40
Dried peanuts (1 ounce)	30

Chapter 9
FOOD FOR THOUGHT

I don't have lots of time to spend shopping for food and making healthy meals. What can I do?

▼
TIP:

Here are some tips:

- Plan your meals for the week, using your diabetes meal plan as a guide. Do all your grocery shopping at once.
- Make a shopping list and move through the store quickly.
- Grated, chopped, precooked, and presliced foods will save preparation time. For example, use prechopped broccoli florets from the salad bar.
- "Cook once, serve two or three times." Plan to use leftovers. For example, if you are making pasta for a hot dish at supper, cook an extra handful to use in a cold pasta salad tomorrow. Make a pot roast with vegetables on Sunday and plan to use the leftover beef in beef stew, burritos, or vegetable beef soup later in the week.
- Take a few minutes in the morning to assemble a slow-cooker recipe. Your reward: a ready-to-eat meal at the end of the day.
- Take advantage of the time you have on weekends. Cook and bake in large quantities and freeze portions for future meals and snacks.

How can I make my favorite recipes lower in fat?

▼
TIP:

These tips may help:

- Most recipes (except some baked goods) will taste fine if you cut 1/3–1/2 of the butter or oil.
- When baking, substitute 2 egg whites for a whole egg; use fat-free instead of whole milk. Reduced-calorie butter or margarine has too much water to be used for baking. Because fat gives texture to baked goods, decreasing it can be tricky. Try replacing oil, margarine, or butter with applesauce. Use an equal amount of fruit for fat to retain moisture and flavor. Puréed prunes taste great in chocolate desserts.
- Marinades need acid, such as lemon juice, vinegar, or wine, more than oil for tenderizing.
- Use lower-fat substitutes. Low-fat yogurt replaces sour cream in dips and dressings. Use evaporated fat-free milk instead of heavy cream. Replace half the ground meat in casseroles with mashed beans or cooked brown rice.
- Use butter-flavored spray on cooked vegetables, baked potatoes, or popcorn.
- Cocoa powder gives chocolate flavor without the fat. Use 3 Tbsp unsweetened cocoa powder and 1 Tbsp vegetable oil to replace 1 oz unsweetened chocolate.

How can I eat right on a lean budget?

▼
TIP:

You don't need expensive diabetic or sugar-free foods. The foundation foods of your meal plan are inexpensive—beans, rice, and whole-grain breads. For snacks, try popcorn, pretzels, and cereal.

Fresh vegetables in season are a great buy. Otherwise, canned, fresh, and frozen vegetables are all quite similar nutritionally. Or, you can grow or pick your own!

Buy fruits in season for best taste and bargain prices. Try the local farmer's market. Think about the cost per serving—if apples and melon are the same price per pound, buy the apples. You throw away the rind of the melon, getting less fruit for the price.

Use fat-free dry milk for cooking and baking. It's inexpensive and stays fresh for a long time if the box is refrigerated. Preshredded cheese saves time but costs more. Buy cheese in blocks and grate it yourself. Buy or make plain yogurt and add your own fresh fruit.

Make meat a side dish, rather than the whole meal. Enjoy meatless meals several times a week. Use leftovers wisely.

Choosing fats, sweets, and alcohol less often will be good for your diabetes and your budget.

Which frozen dessert is best for me?

▼
TIP:

You can eat frozen desserts occasionally if you substitute them for other carbohydrates in your meal plan. The following information can help you choose:

- Watch the serving size (1/2 cup). If you eat more, double or triple the nutrient information to keep your count accurate.
- Watch the fat content, particularly the saturated fat. Light ice cream or yogurt contains about half the fat of the regular kind. Fat-free ice cream still has sugar, carbohydrate, and calories.
- A no-sugar-added frozen dessert may still contain carbohydrate, fat, and calories. Sweeteners commonly used in frozen desserts include aspartame and sugar alcohols such as sorbitol (see p. 57).
- Check your blood glucose after eating a frozen dessert to see how it affects you.

Frozen Dessert (1/2 cup)	Calories	Carbohydrate (g)	Fat (g)	Saturated Fat (g)
Regular ice cream	133	16	7	7
Light ice cream	100	14	4	3
Fat-free ice cream	90	20	0	0
No-sugar-added ice cream	100	13	4	3
Sherbet	132	29	2	1
Sorbet	92	23	0	0

Are frozen dinners a good choice for quick meals?

▼
TIP:

Frozen dinners have come a long way, but keep the following tips in mind:

- Check the Nutrition Facts panel for the amount of fat and sodium. You want no more than 30% of calories from fat, 10% of calories from saturated fat, and 200 mg of sodium for every 100 calories.
- Most "healthy" frozen dinners are based on small servings. If your meal plan calls for 1,500 calories a day, don't skimp by eating a meal with less than 400 or 500 calories. You'll find yourself hungry later and may overeat on snacks.
- Be aware that although most healthy frozen dinners contain fruits and vegetables, the serving size of these foods is as small as 1 tablespoon in some cases.

You can improve a frozen dinner by adding a salad, some steamed vegetables, and a piece of fruit. It may be better to make your own frozen dinners by putting the extras from home-cooked meals onto microwave safe dishes in your serving sizes.

Are eggs off-limits now that I have diabetes?

▼
TIP:

No. Contrary to the widely held belief that cholesterol-rich eggs are bad for heart health, several research studies have found that for most people, dietary cholesterol has little effect on the cholesterol level in blood. Saturated fat has a more significant effect on your blood cholesterol level (see p. 42). A person's response to dietary cholesterol is highly individual and genetically determined. About 20% of us have little or no response to dietary cholesterol, 50% show a small response, and the remaining 30% are responders, particularly sensitive to high-cholesterol foods. There is no easy test to determine who is cholesterol sensitive, so just be cautious when using eggs and other cholesterol-rich foods.

An egg is an economical source of protein, providing 70 calories, less than 1 gram of carbohydrate, 4.5 grams of fat, and 1 gram of saturated fat. One egg contains vitamins, minerals, and about 215 mg of cholesterol.

Don't eliminate eggs from your diet. Use them wisely or follow the American Heart Association guideline—no more than four a week.

How can I use herbs and spices?

▼
TIP:

Herbs and spices taste good, smell good, and best of all, have no effect on diabetes control. They are free foods on every meal plan. Herbs and spices come fresh or dried. Dried herbs have more intense flavor. (When substituting fresh for dried herbs, double or triple the amount.) The amount of herb or spice that you use in a recipe depends on individual taste.

Here is a list of traditional spice partners:

- Beef: bay leaf, chives, garlic, marjoram, savory
- Lamb: garlic, marjoram, mint, oregano, rosemary, sage, savory
- Pork: cilantro, cumin, ginger, sage, thyme
- Poultry: garlic, oregano, rosemary, sage, thyme
- Seafood: chervil, dill weed, fennel, tarragon, parsley
- Pasta: basil, oregano, fennel, garlic, paprika, parsley, sage
- Rice: marjoram, parsley, tarragon, thyme, turmeric
- Potatoes: chives, garlic, paprika, parsley, rosemary
- Fruits: cinnamon, cloves, ginger, mint
- Salads: basil, chervil, chives, dill weed, marjoram, mint, oregano, parsley, tarragon, thyme

Be aware that some herb blends contain sodium or are salts, such as garlic salt or lemon pepper.

Chapter 10
SPECIAL SITUATIONS

What should I use to treat low blood glucose?

▼
TIP:

Always carry something with you to treat low blood glucose. Do not use chocolate or candy bars because they may not bring your blood glucose up quickly enough.

1. Check your blood glucose. If it is below 70 mg/dl or you have signs of hypoglycemia but cannot test, eat one of the foods below.
2. Rest for 15 minutes and retest your blood glucose.
3. If it is still low, eat another treatment food and retest. If it is normal, go to the next step.
4. After treating your low blood glucose, eat an extra snack with about 15 grams of carbohydrate. If a meal or snack is scheduled within an hour, go ahead and eat it now.
5. Get help immediately if your blood glucose is still low after 30 minutes and 2 treatments.

Low Blood Glucose Treatment Foods (15 g carbohydrate)	
1/2 cup juice or regular soft drink	10 jelly beans
1 Tbsp honey	8 LifeSavers
4 tsp sugar	2 Tbsp raisins
3 pieces of hard candy	Glucose or dextrose tablets or gel

What foods can I eat when I am sick?

▼

TIP:

When you are sick, take your usual medication, check your blood glucose, and test your urine for ketones. If you can't eat regular food, have carbohydrates in liquids or soft foods. Drink plenty of fluids—at least 4–6 oz every hour. If you can't eat at your usual times, have 15 g carbohydrate every hour to keep blood glucose from dropping. (See list below.)

These tips can help you handle sick days:

- Sip clear liquids, such as apple juice, sports drinks, or regular soda, if you can't keep anything else down.
- Use broth, vegetable juices, and sports drinks to replace potassium and sodium lost from diarrhea and vomiting.
- Ask your RD for sick-day meal plans.

Sick-Day Foods (15 g carbohydrate)	
1 cup broth soup	1/4 cup sherbet
1 cup cream soup	1/2 cup regular soda
1/2 cup fruit juice	1 small frozen juice bar
1 cup milk or yogurt	1 cup sports drink
1/3 cup plain pudding	1/2 cup unsweetened applesauce
1/2 cup ice milk or ice cream	6 saltines
1/2 cup regular gelati	

Can I safely drink alcohol?

▼
TIP:

It depends. Alcohol can make blood glucose too high or too low. Eat a meal when you drink alcohol to prevent low blood glucose. Alcoholic beverages with mixers, wine, and beer have carbohydrates and can cause your blood glucose to go too high. Choose lower calorie mixers such as mineral water, club soda, diet tonic water, diet soda, coffee, or tomato juice. Choose light beer or a glass of wine.

If your diabetes is in control, you may have a moderate amount of alcohol—one drink each day. One drink is a 12-oz beer, 5 oz of wine, or 1 1/2 oz of liquor. If you have type 1 diabetes and you are not overweight, this serving would be an addition to your meal plan. If you have type 2 diabetes or are overweight, any alcohol you drink should be substituted for another food in your meal plan. Ask your RD for help.

Avoid alcohol if your blood glucose is out of control, you have an empty stomach, you are pregnant, have neuropathy, have problems with alcohol abuse, take prescription or over-the-counter medications that react with alcohol, or have just had vigorous exercise.

How can I eat less fat when I eat out in restaurants?

▼
TIP:

Identify your habits by answering these questions:

- How often do you eat out?
- What meals do you eat out most often?
- What type of restaurants do you choose most often?
- What foods do you order?

Select restaurants that have some lower-fat choices. Get copies of menus and decide what you will eat before you arrive. Plan ways to balance your restaurant meal with food choices the rest of the day. Save fat choices for your meal out.

Choose menu items or foods that are baked, braised, broiled, grilled, poached, roasted, steamed, or stir-fried instead of au gratin, fried, breaded, buttered, creamed, sautéed, scalloped, or with gravy or thick sauce. Look for menu items called *light* or *lean.* Ask about food preparation and ingredients. Ask that sauces and salad dressings be served on the side. Decline any extra bread or tortilla chips.

If a serving seems too big, order an appetizer instead, split a main dish with your dining companion, or take home leftovers. Set aside the portion you want to take home as soon as the food arrives.

Which fast foods can I eat?

TIP:

The following tips can help you decide:

- Watch the serving size. Order a regular serving or split the super-size with someone.
- Most restaurants have free nutrient information. Ask for it.
- Go for grilled, broiled, baked, or rotisserie sandwiches. Skip meats with breading and cheese.
- Remember your fruits and vegetables. Order juice or fruit, a salad or raw vegetables, tomato slices or vegetables for sandwiches, vegetable toppings for potatoes, or vegetables on pizza.
- Bagels, muffins, French fries, baked potatoes, and sandwich buns can be extra large and give you too much carbohydrate. Cut them in half or split an order.
- Low-fat frozen yogurt, low-fat milk shakes, and fresh fruit are good dessert choices. Order small sizes or share.
- For breakfast, order cereal, English muffins, fruit, and milk.
- Ask that catsup, barbecue sauce, mayonnaise, salad dressing, tartar sauce, honey, cream cheese, and others be left off your sandwich or salad.

How can I avoid overeating at a salad bar or buffet?

▼
TIP:

An average plate from the salad bar can give you more than 1,000 calories, depending on choices and portions. Consider these tips:

- Don't go to restaurants that only offer buffet-style eating or salad bar.
- Take a stroll around the salad bar, breakfast bar, or buffet to size up your choices before you decide.
- If you are tempted to overdo, use a smaller plate. Single trips are usually less expensive.
- Enjoy plenty of vegetables, legumes (such as kidney and garbanzo beans), and fresh fruit.
- Dark green leafy vegetables (such as spinach and romaine) supply more vitamins than iceberg lettuce. Choose fresh fruit instead of juice or sweet breads at breakfast bars.
- Become familiar with calories and fat in typical salad bar foods. A 2-Tbsp ladle of salad dressing adds 150 calories to a salad. Choose low-fat or fat-free salad dressing.
- Side dishes such as potato salad, pasta salad, and creamy soups add calories and fat quickly. Avoid these or take small servings of less than 1 Tbsp.

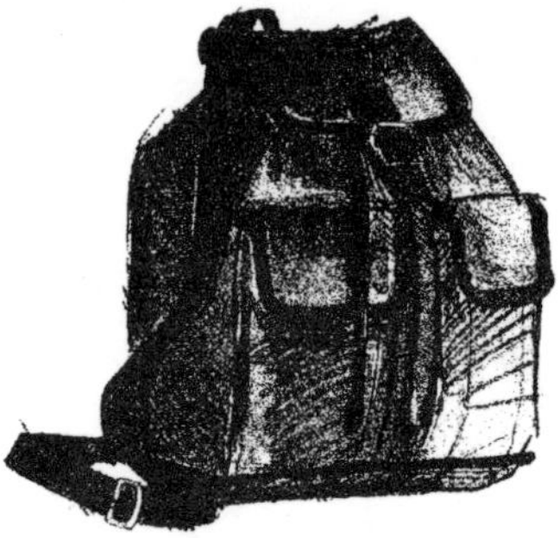

What do I do if my meal is delayed for an hour?

▼

TIP:

Don't let your blood glucose get too low. If your scheduled meal is delayed for an hour, take your diabetes medication at your usual time before the meal. Then eat 15 g of carbohydrate at your usual mealtime. Always keep quick and easy carbohydrate foods (see ideas below) with you in your purse, briefcase, locker, glove compartment, or backpack. Eat your dinner when it is ready.

For meals that are delayed for more than 1 1/2 hours, adjustments depend on when and what kind of diabetes medications you take. Many times you can switch a snack with a meal. Check with your diabetes professionals for a specific plan.

Emergency Foods (15 g carbohydrate)	
6 saltines	1/2 oz dried fruit
2 rice cakes	3 prunes
3/4 oz pretzels	cereal bars (may be more than 15 g)
3 graham crackers	

How can I eat healthy when I travel on the airlines?

▼
TIP:

The following tips should help:

- If the airline meal won't fit your meal plan, bring your own. Having food with you is essential for any kind of travel.
- If a meal is to be served, call your agent or airline several days before the flight and order a special meal. Major airlines offer free diabetic, vegetarian, low-calorie, low-fat, and low-sodium meals. When you board, tell the flight attendant that you ordered a special meal and need it on time. After your meal arrives, take your diabetes medication. If your special meal isn't available, eat the regular meal and substitute other food that you have brought. Foods such as bagels, cereal, fruit, crackers, cheese, raisins, and bottled water travel easily.
- Drink plenty of liquids before, during, and after the flight to avoid dehydration and jet lag. Beverage choices include milk, vegetable and fruit juice, and bottled water. Don't drink too many caffeinated beverages.
- Check your blood glucose. Your activity level during airline travel is low, so you may need to adjust your meal plan or medication. For help, contact your RD.

How can I keep my weight and blood glucose levels in control during the holiday season?

▼
TIP:

You can keep your holiday spirit by using the following tips:

- **Holiday meals:** Thanksgiving dinner can add up to 4,500 calories if you include appetizers, eggnog, turkey, trimmings, and dessert. Redesign dinner with delicious lower-fat dishes. Serve grain, fruit, and vegetable dishes. Substitute white turkey meat for dark meat; make your own cranberry sauce; skim the fat off the gravy.
- **Holiday parties:** Have a small snack before you go. Don't socialize by the food table, but do socialize. For potlucks, bring a dish you know you can enjoy. Watch the alcohol; it can lower your resistance to tempting treats.
- **Holiday travel:** Pack healthy, portable snacks to see you through the trip. Good ones include fresh or dried fruit, pretzels, low-fat chips, ready-to-eat cereal, and low-fat cheese (see p. 101).

Take advantage of opportunities for exercise. Walk the mall before you shop or take a stroll with your family after dinner to see neighborhood decorations. Keep things in perspective, and if you overindulge, make good choices the rest of the year.

How do I adjust food and insulin for a swing-shift schedule?

▼
TIP:

Your RD and physician must help you plan insulin doses, mealtimes, and physical activities. Multiple daily injections are usually recommended. Learning to adjust rapid-acting insulin to your meal size and carbohydrate content (see pp. 17, 31) gives you flexibility for unpredictable meals. Frequent blood glucose monitoring on workdays and days off helps you make adjustments. Your activity varies from workdays to days off, so your food and/or insulin need adjustments then, too.

If you work the 11 P.M.–7 A.M. shift, try this:

1. Eat before you go to work and take rapid-acting insulin and intermediate- or long-acting insulin (usual before breakfast injections).
2. Eat your next meal around 3:00 A.M. and take rapid-acting insulin.
3. Eat a snack, if needed, between 3:00 –7:00 A.M.
4. Eat a meal at home 8:00–8:30 A.M. and take rapid-acting insulin and intermediate- or long-acting insulin (usual before dinner injections).
5. Sleep between 9:00 A.M.–4:00 P.M.
6. Eat a snack between 5:00–8:00 P.M.

Should I use a slow-release carbohydrate snack bar to prevent hypoglycemia?

▼
TIP:

Products such as Zbar and Nite Bite are medical foods that reduce hypoglycemia for hours, particularly at night. These snack bars are based on a long-acting carbohydrate (such as cornstarch) and come in fruit flavors, chocolate crunch, and peanut butter.

These bars were developed when researchers found that in children with glycogen storage disease and hypoglycemia, blood glucose levels could be stabilized for nine hours by feeding uncooked cornstarch. This was also true in children with diabetes who followed an intensive insulin regimen. Snack bars were created as a tasty alternative to plain cornstarch.

The Diabetes Control and Complications Trial (DCCT) showed that hypoglycemia accompanies tight diabetes control. If you are taking multiple daily insulin injections, these bars may help you. They contain 22 grams of carbohydrate per bar (1 1/2 starch exchanges) and are added to an evening snack to reduce the risk of nighttime and early morning hypoglycemia. Blood glucose monitoring will help you determine the effect these snack bars have on you. Consider the cost and taste, and discuss using them with your diabetes care providers.

Do I need to drink a nutritional supplement now that I'm a senior?

▼ **TIP:**

Maybe. For some people, keeping a balance of nutrients may be more difficult because calorie needs decrease with aging, food budgets get tight, appetite decreases, social contact is reduced, or eating problems arise.

If you are in good health and have a varied diet, you probably don't need these supplement drinks. Some people use them for convenience. Check the Nutrition Facts panel for calories, carbohydrate, protein, and fat content. Some are high in sugar. Ask your RD whether these drinks fit your meal plan. Monitor your blood glucose levels when you use these nutrition drinks to see how they affect your diabetes. You may not be able to find these products in stores near you, or they may be too expensive for your budget. Ask your RD about supplemental drinks you can make at home. If you are concerned about being underweight, ask for high-calorie meal ideas, too. Try eating five or six small meals a day.

Chapter 11
NUTRITION POTPOURRI

Does cow's milk cause type 1 diabetes?

TIP:

The answer remains a mystery. Researchers are studying early exposure to cow's milk (before age 3–4 months) as a cause of type 1 diabetes. Infant formulas are made from cow's milk. Children with type 1 diabetes have shown higher amounts of antibodies that recognize a specific protein in cow's milk. The immune response to the milk proteins might be related to the destruction of insulin-producing beta cells in the pancreas and to type 1 diabetes. Other studies have not found this same link between cow's milk and type 1 diabetes.

Breast milk is the best source of nutrition during the first year of life for infants with or without diabetes. Breast milk offers physical, emotional, and practical benefits. The baby benefits even when breastfed for only a short time.

However, breastfeeding may not be right for every woman. Commercial infant formula is a healthful alternative or supplement to breastfeeding. The cow's milk used to make infant formula has been modified to meet an infant's special needs. The decision to breastfeed or use commercial infant formula is a personal one. Discuss questions or concerns with your diabetes professionals and your pediatrician.

Will becoming a vegetarian help my diabetes control?

▼
TIP:

Yes, a vegetarian diet can be a healthy choice for people with diabetes. There are several types of vegetarian diets.

- **Lacto-ovo-vegetarian:** no flesh foods, including meat, fish, seafood, poultry and their byproducts, but includes some dairy products and eggs
- **Lacto-vegetarian:** no flesh foods, eggs, and their byproducts, but includes some dairy products
- **Vegan:** no foods of animal origin

Vegetarian diets are based on fruits, vegetables, grains, beans, lentils, soybeans, nuts, and seeds. As a result, they are low in fat, cholesterol, and calories. Decreasing your use of animal products offers you several diabetes health advantages. Vegetarians are less likely to be overweight, have high cholesterol levels, or to have high blood pressure. They are also less likely to suffer from heart and blood vessel disease and certain cancers. If you have type 1 diabetes, becoming a vegetarian may enable you to use less insulin. If you have type 2 diabetes, the weight loss from a vegetarian diet may improve your blood glucose control. An RD can help you plan vegetarian meals and ensure that you get all the vitamins, minerals, and protein you need.

I binge-eat under stress. How can I avoid overeating the next time I feel pressured?

TIP:

Learn the difference between hunger and appetite. Hunger is a physical sensation that tells you that your body needs food. Appetite comes from the mind and is triggered by sensation and emotion. The following are several ways to deal with the urge to "stuff your feelings" or binge:

- Identify the situations that cause you to overeat. Keep a diary of how much you eat, when you eat, and what the triggers are.
- Establish regular eating patterns. Skipping meals or not eating enough leads to overeating.
- Limit foods that tempt you. If it's chocolate, don't bring full-sized candy bars into the house; a fun-sized bar may satisfy the craving.
- Change the ways you cope with stress. Rather than eat,
  - Exercise. Being active (walking, biking) is good for your mind and your body.
  - Talk with a supportive friend or family member.
  - Enjoy a warm bath or long shower.
  - Take good care of yourself. Listen to music you enjoy, go to a movie, get a massage.

Stress can affect your blood glucose in several ways. Discuss your reactions to stress with your health care team.

Should I follow a low-sodium diet?

▼
TIP:

Most people aren't affected by excess sodium. However, if you are one of the 30% of Americans who have sodium-sensitive blood pressure, decreasing sodium intake will reduce your blood pressure.

People with diabetes have the same recommended sodium intake as the general population, 2,400–3,000 mg per day. People with mild to moderate high blood pressure should have less than 2,400 mg. People with high blood pressure and kidney disease should eat less than 2,000 mg per day.

To lower your sodium intake

- Check Nutrition Facts for sodium.
- Don't use processed foods. Buy fresh meats, fruits, and vegetables instead of high-salt meat products (bacon, cold cuts, ham), canned soups, or frozen dinners.
- Be cautious with condiments and sauces. Cut back on pickles, ketchup, soy sauce, salad dressing, steak sauce, and teriyaki sauce.
- Cook with less salt. Try herbs, spices, lemon juice, pepper, or garlic (see p. 92).
- Remove the salt shaker from the table. Taste food before salting.
- Avoid high-sodium menu items. Recognize them by description (smoked or in broth). Keep your order simple (without sauces or fillings) and request that it be prepared without added salt.

I have gastroparesis. What changes do I make in my diet?

▼
TIP:

Your stomach has lost the ability to churn food into small pieces, and food stays in the stomach too long. Symptoms include nausea, vomiting, weight loss, and a feeling of bloating and fullness. Your blood glucose level may be difficult to control because food is not delivered to the small intestine for absorption in time to match the diabetes medication you take. You may need medication that stimulates your stomach to contract and empty.

As for your diet, you may need to

- Eat small meals over the day rather than one or two large meals
- Avoid fatty foods because fat slows stomach emptying
- Avoid foods that are difficult to digest such as legumes, lentils, and citrus fruits

Because high blood glucose levels can also slow stomach emptying, getting blood glucose levels under control is an important part of treatment. If you are taking insulin, your diabetes team may suggest intensive insulin therapy (an insulin pump or three or more injections a day) and frequent blood glucose monitoring. You may need to take your insulin after you eat because of the unpredictability of food absorption.

My father has type 2 diabete and I'm worried I will get it, too. Is there a diet I can follov to prevent getting diabetes?

▼
TIP:

Yes, a healthy diet with regular exercise. Type 2 diabetes is probably caused by a hereditary defect that reduces a person's sensitivity to insulin. You can't change that, but you can change the lifestyle (high-calorie diet and inactive sedentary) habits that can lead to obesity, which is the most important environmental trigger of type 2 diabetes. This is why diet and exercise are the major part of prevention and treatment.

Government research studies (The Diabetes Prevention Program) are studying the effects of lifestyle changes and medication in preventing or delaying the development of type 2 diabetes. Participants in the intensive lifestyle group follow a healthy low-fat diet and regular exercise habits to achieve weight loss.

Until the results of this study are available, it's best to change you lifestyle to achieve or maintain a healthy weight. Talk with your health care providers about starting a low-fat diet and increasing you physical activity. An RD can help you learn about healthy eating and your exercise program.

Chapter 12
RESOURCES

The following books are available at bookstores nationwide, or they can be ordered from the publisher.

A Guide to Fitting Foods with Sugar Substitutes and Fat Replacers into Your Meal Plan. American Diabetes Association, 1998.

American Diabetes Association Complete Guide to Diabetes. American Diabetes Association, 1996.

Being Vegetarian: Up-to-Date Tips from the World's Foremost Nutrition Experts. Chronimed Publishing, 1996.

Carbohydrate Counting: Getting Started; Moving On; Using Carbohydrate/Insulin Ratios. The American Dietetic Association and American Diabetes Association, 1995.

Dear Diabetes Advisor. American Diabetes Association, 1997.

Diabetes A to Z. American Diabetes Association, 1997.

Diabetes Meal Planning Made Easy. Hope Warshaw, MMSc, RD, CDE. American Diabetes Association, 1996.

Diabetes Meal Planning on $7 a Day—or Less. Patti B. Geil, MS, RD, FADA, CDE, and Tami A. Ross, RD, CDE. American Diabetes Association, 1999.

How to Cook for People with Diabetes. American Diabetes Association, 1996.

Magic Beans: 150 Recipes Featuring Nature's Low-Fat, Nutrient-Rich, Disease-Fighting Powerhouse. Patti Bazel Geil, MS, RD, CDE. Chronimed Publishing, 1996.

Month of Meals: Vegetarian Pleasures. American Diabetes Association, 1998.

Quick & Easy Diabetic Recipes for One. Kathleen Stanley, CDE, RD, MSEd, and Connie Crawley, MS, RD, LD. American Diabetes Association, 1997.

Reading Food Labels: A Handbook for People with Diabetes. American Diabetes Association, 1994.

Skim the Fat. The American Dietetic Association. Chronimed Publishing, 1995.

Sweet Kids: How to Balance Diabetes Control & Good Nutrition with Family Peace. Betty Brackenridge, RD, and Richard Rubin, PhD. American Diabetes Association, 1996.

The Bean Bag. Newsletter of The Michigan Bean Commission. 1031 South US 27, St. Johns, MI 48879.

The Carbohydrate Counting Cookbook. Tami Ross, RD, CDE, and Patti B. Geil, MS, RD, FADA, CDE. Chronimed Publishing, 1998.

The Chef's Guide to Herbs & Spices. Lea Ann Holzmeister, RD, CDE. Diabetes Self-Management Books, 1994.

The Commonsense Guide to Weight Loss for People with Diabetes. Barbara Hansen, PhD, and Shauna Roberts, PhD. American Diabetes Association, 1998.

The Complete Weight Loss Workbook. Judith Wylie-Rosett, EdD, RD, et al. American Diabetes Association, 1998.

The Diabetes Carbohydrate and Fat Gram Guide. Lea Ann Holzmeister, RD, CDE. American Diabetes Association and The American Dietetic Association, 1997.

The Diabetes Snack Munch Nibble Nosh Book. Ruth Glick. American Diabetes Association, 1998.

Exchange Lists for Meal Planning. The American Dietetic Association and American Diabetes Association, 1995.

The First Step in Diabetes Meal Planning. American Diabetes Association and The American Dietetic Association, 1995.

The Fitness Book for People with Diabetes. American Diabetes Association, 1994.

The American Diabetes Association Guide to Healthy Restaurant Eating for People with Diabetes. Hope Warshaw, MMSc, RD, CDE. American Diabetes Association, 1998.

The Official Pocket Guide to Diabetic Exchanges. American Diabetes Association, 1998.

The Uncomplicated Guide to Diabetes Complications. Marvin E. Levin, MD, and Michael Pfeifer, MD, Eds. American Diabetes Association, 1998.

Type 2 Diabetes: Your Healthy Living Guide. American Diabetes Association, 1997.

Vegetarian Beginner's Guide. Vegetarian Times, 1996.

When Diabetes Hits Home. Wendy Satin Rapaport, LCSW, PsyD. American Diabetes Association, 1998.

American Association of Diabetes Educators (AADE) (800) 832-687
444 N. Michigan Avenue (312) 644-223
Suite 1240
Chicago, IL 60611-3901

American Diabetes Association (800) 342-2383 (information
1660 Duke Street (800) 806-7801 (membership
Alexandria, VA 22314 (800) 232-6733 (books
www.diabetes.org
bookstore: merchant.diabetes.org

The American Dietetic Association (800) 366-165
216 West Jackson Blvd.
Suite 800
Chicago, IL 60606-6995
www.eatright.org

World Wide Web Sites
www.dole5aday.com
www.soyfoods.com

INDEX

W

Y

Z